Why the *Lyrical Ballads*?

WHY THE
Lyrical Ballads
?

THE
BACKGROUND, WRITING,
AND CHARACTER OF WORDSWORTH'S
1798 *LYRICAL BALLADS*

by
JOHN E. JORDAN

UNIVERSITY OF CALIFORNIA PRESS
BERKELEY   LOS ANGELES   LONDON

To the memory of
HUGH DeSHAZO JORDAN
28 September 1956—8 December 1974

University of California Press
Berkeley and Los Angeles, California
University of California Press, Ltd.
London, England
Copyright © 1976 by
The Regents of the University of California
ISBN 0-520-03124-5
Library of Congress Catalog Card Number: 75-27926
Printed in the United States of America

CONTENTS

CONTENTS

PREFACE

LAMB once remarked that he did not need to write a Preface, because a Preface was just a chance for an author to talk to his readers, and he did that throughout. Without pretending to Lamb's gift of intimacy, this book hopes to talk to readers. Nevertheless, perhaps it needs a Preface, to explain its title if for no other reason.

Much has been written about the *Lyrical Ballads* and Wordsworth's early poetry in general. Like other Wordsworthians, I am grateful for such studies as John F. Danby's *The Simple Wordsworth: Studies in the Poems of 1797-1807* (London, 1906), Roger N. Murray's *Wordsworth's Style: Figures and Themes in the Lyrical Ballads of 1800* (University of Nebraska Press, 1967), Jared R. Curtis' *Wordsworth's Experiments with Tradition: The Lyric Poems of 1802* (Cornell University Press, 1971), Paul D. Sheats' *The Making of Wordsworth's Poetry, 1785-1798* (Harvard University Press, 1973), and Stephen Maxfield Parrish's *The Art of the Lyrical Ballads* (Harvard University Press, 1973), as well as the work of Charles Ryskamp, Albert S. Gérard, James Benziger, Stephen Gill, Roger Sharrock, M.H. Abrams, Mark Reed, Jonathan Woodsworth, and Mary Jacobus. But no study I know of has yet addressed itself to the whole question of how and why the *Lyrical Ballads* evolved and took the form of the first edition. I do not pretend to answer all these questions, but I am fascinated by the number of interrelated *why's*, particularly as they concern Wordsworth's

vii

central contributions to the first edition of the *Lyrical Ballads*.

Pervasively, there is the question of literary history: *Why* has the *Lyrical Ballads* traditionally been considered a landmark? Was it a signal new departure, or was it—as has more recently been suggested by Robert Mayo—more or less conventional in its day? This *why* leads to a series of questions about the literary environment and thus the novelty, the originality (and inevitably, the reception) of the *Lyrical Ballads*, and therefore its relationship to the contemporary fad of "simplicity."

Then there are the questions of *why* and how the little book got written—what were the motivations behind it and the literary theories and attitudes which informed it from the beginning? These questions are more complicated than is sometimes taken for granted because of the tendency to rely upon the Preface—which was attached to the two-volume second edition of 1800 and significantly modified in 1802—and upon Coleridge's still later comments in the *Biographia Literaria* (1817). Then come the related *why's* and hows of the publication of the slim anonymous issue of a provincial press. *Why* did the volume take the form it did? The result is probably less a matter of a division of labor between Wordsworth and Coleridge, or the developing of a "curse" theme, than it is of the need to get funds for a trip to Germany and the fussy urgings of that pompous busy-body publisher and discoverer-protector of the poets, Joseph Cottle.

Finally there is the curiously nagging question of *why* the little book was given its famous title. We may be tempted to dismiss that question as relatively unimportant, a matter of idle curiosity—especially since it is a very difficult question, for which a perfect answer can probably never be given. But in a sense it is the heart of the matter—what is a "lyrical ballad"? What is the special quality of the poems Wordsworth wrote in 1798; what impulse led him to create a "stock" of poems to contribute to the collaboration with Coleridge, and what did he mean by calling them "lyrical ballads"?

The arrangement of chapters in this book begins with a narrative order, but invokes flashbacks to the events. We first follow the writing and publishing of the 1798 *Lyrical Ballads*; then, in connection with its reception, we go back to the critical environment in which it developed and examine Wordsworth's relation to the contemporary shibboleth of the "simple." The larger view of the critical reception leads to considering Wordsworth's perception of the novelty of the enterprise and its originality when judged by comparison with other verse being published at the time. Then we consider Wordsworth's purpose in writing the "lyrical ballads" and his intent in so naming them.

A version of Chapter Five was published in *Bicentenary Wordsworth Studies in Memory of John Alban French*, edited by Jonathan Wordsworth and Beth Darlington (Cornell, 1970), pp. 340-358, and is used here with the permission of the Univ. of Cornell Press. Part of Chapter Four was read at a meeting of Section Nine of the Modern Language Association, and part of Chapter Six at the first Wordsworth Conference at Rydal Mount; other segments have been offered to the Berkeley English Conference, the Kosmos Club, and my students. I am grateful for all the contributions and comments added in the process by editors and auditors.

As to my other indebtedness, I hardly know where to begin. A work like this has been built up slowly over many years of working in libraries. I am especially conscious of the courtesies extended me by the Huntington Library, the Rare Book Room of the University of Illinois

Library, the British Museum, the University of Cambridge Library, the Bodleian Library, the Dove Cottage Wordsworth Library, and of course the University of California Library. For various kinds of encouragement and assistance, I should like to express my gratitude to Patricia Pelfrey, Ulrich Knoepflmacher, Paul Sheats, Carl Woodring, and Director August Frugé of the University of California Press.

ABBREVIATIONS
USED IN TEXT AND NOTES

EY	*The Letters of William and Dorothy Wordsworth; The Early Years: 1787-1805*, ed. Ernest De Selincourt, Second Edition revised by Chester L. Shaver (Oxford, 1967).
Howe	*The Complete works of William Hazlitt*, ed. P.P. Howe, 21 vols. (London, 1930-1934).
Letters	*Collected Letters of Samuel Taylor Coleridge*, ed. Earl Leslie Griggs, 6 vols. (Oxford, 1956-1971).
LY	*The Letters of William and Dorothy Wordsworth; The Later Years: 1821-1850*, ed.
Moorman	Mary Moorman, *William Wordsworth: A Biography—The Early Years: 1770-1803* (Oxford, 1957).
MY	*The Letters of William and Dorothy Wordsworth, II and III; The Middle Years: Part I, 1806-1811; Part II, 1812-1820*, ed. Ernest De Selincourt, Second Edition revised by Mary Moorman and Alan G. Hill (Oxford, 1969-1970).
Prose Wks.	*The Prose Works of William Wordsworth*, ed. W. J. B. Owen and Jane Worthington Smyser, 3 vols. (Oxford, 1974).

PW   *The Poetical Works of William Wordsworth*,
              ed. E. De Selincourt and Helen Darbishire,
              5 vols. (Oxford, 1940-1952).

Reed, *CEY*   Mark L. Reed, *Wordsworth, The Chronol-
              ogy of the Early Years: 1770-1799* (Harvard
              University Press, 1967).

Reed, *CMY*   Mark L. Reed, *Wordsworth, The Chronol-
              ogy of the Middle Years: 1800-1815* (Harvard
              University Press, 1975).

INTRODUCTION
AND
CONCLUSION

BECAUSE this book is aimed at supplying information and answering a series of *why's*, it does not have a neat thesis. In nearly every area of consideration, we find complexity: dualistic standards, mixed motives. Yet the *why's* seem to keep getting similar answers in different areas. There seems to be a common resonance, a resonance which is also central to a famous passage from perhaps the best-known poem in the *Lyrical Ballads*:

> And I have felt
> A presence that disturbs me with the joy
> Of elevated thoughts; a sense sublime
> Of something far more deeply interfused,
> Whose dwelling is the light of setting suns,
> And the round ocean and the living air,
> And the blue sky, and in the mind of man:
> (*Tintern Abbey*, 93-9)

This book does not say much about "Lines Composed a few miles above Tintern Abbey, on Revisiting the Banks of the Wye during a Tour. July 13, 1798," partly because so much has been said about it already, and partly because it was the last poem to go into the first edition of the *Lyrical Ballads* and has to be regarded as more of an afterthought than part of the core of the experiment. Although Wordsworth did not call it an ode, he seems to have thought of it as such;[1] it is undoubtedly one of the "few other poems" referred to in the full title of the volume, and therefore not really a "lyrical ballad" at all.

1

But because of its terminal and climactic position in the collection, this poem may cast a special light back on the project. We may therefore gain some illumination from looking at the quoted passage as a convenient focus of certain ideas that will be seen to resonate through our varied approaches to the *Lyrical Ballads*. Also this passage is especially valuable in reminding us that the close particularity signaled by the specific date in the poem's title, and the autobiographical strain which runs through the poem, are not completely characteristic of Wordsworth's poetic impulse at the time of the famous experiment.

If we put aside the usual arguments as to how far this passage is pantheistic, and emphasize instead its philosophical implications, we find that it expresses ideas central to the view of life which directed Wordsworth's thinking at the time he was writing the *Lyrical Ballads*—and for that matter remained significant in his subsequent work. The central idea of this passage is pervasive, enduring, essential universality, a "sense sublime" of something which although it is said to be in "motion" carries a static sense of ubiquitous, permanent being. Perhaps it is worth reminding ourselves that in the 1800 Preface to *Lyrical Ballads* Wordsworth underlined his concern with "permanent forms" and "permanent" language, with "elementary feelings" and "durable" manners, and in 1802 added a definition of poetry which asserts "its object is truth, not individual and local, but general, and operative." It is also significant that in a letter written to Sir George Beaumont in 1808 he protested that a friend of the baronet's had referred to one of Wordsworth's pieces as "a poem on a Daisy," because in fact "it is on *the* Daisy, a mighty difference." The universalized, generic "the" makes a "mighty difference."[2]

Throughout this study we see these universalizing attitudes reflected in various ways. Not only does Wordsworth's relation to the critical environment, and his particular use of the concept of simplicity, bring him to the elemental and universal (Chapters Three and Four), but his very insistence upon the novelty of the experiment proves to be common if not universal in his age, so that even his novelty is not idiosyncratic (Chapter Five). Furthermore, by comparison with contemporary verse, one of the more original aspects of his poems written at this time is his virtual eschewing of the topical in favor of the eternal (Chapter Six); and his purpose in the poems written for *Lyrical Ballads* seems to have been to produce a special kind of description focused upon people feeling, which emphasizes the typical, the common, the universal (Chapter Seven). Finally, his exploitation of the ballad form appears to strive for common psychological insights or (in language that properly magnifies their human significance) "elevated thoughts" couched in superior metrics— which amounts to a universalization of the genre (Chapter Eight). This is a poetry (as Wordsworth says in his note to "The Thorn") which is "the history or science of feelings."

Wordsworth's formulation in this note, which appeared in the 1800-1805 editions, is important; we will refer to it hereafter, but now a look at its implications and tensions:

the Reader cannot be too often reminded that Poetry is passion: it is the history or science of feelings; now every man must know that an attempt is rarely made to communicate impassioned feelings without something of an accompanying consciousness of the inadequateness of our own powers, or the deficiencies of language. (*PW*, II, 513)

If poetry is a "history or science," it follows that it is an objective record having a rational, deductive component. Its special quality is that it is a *record* of *feelings*— an objective, communicable, maybe quantifiable, certainly universalizable record of something regularly associated with emotion, the individual, the unique, maybe even the ineffable. The combination seems almost a romantic "reconciliation of opposites." We should remind ourselves, however, that Wordsworth's contemporary and acquaintance, William Godwin, known as an apostle of reason, declared in the Preface to *An Enquiry concerning the Principles of Political Justice:* "passion is so far from being incompatible with reason that it is inseparable from it." Science can be pursued with passion and become a proper poetic subject; in his 1802 addition to the Preface Wordsworth looked forward to a time when the Poet would carry "sensation into the midst of the objects of the science itself" (*Prose Wks.*, I, 141).[3] Meanwhile, passion can be so broadly based in human experience that it can be rationalized and universalized—and this area was already available to the poet of *Lyrical Ballads.*

Wordsworth was acutely conscious of the paradoxical combination; he fought the pull toward the incommunicable, and was sometimes on the verge of despairing that feelings could be translated into language. The subject matter of his verse was often drawn from the world of "dumb yearnings" (*Prelude*, V, 506), where the deficiencies of language" are most conspicuous. He tells us that he became lost, was left fumbling for words, when on a continental tour he suffered a kind of epiphany upon the realization that he had crossed the Alps and was on his way down:

> Imagination—here the Power so called
> Through sad incompetence of human speech,
> That awful Power rose from the mind's abyss
> Like an unfathered vapour that enwraps,
> At once, some lonely traveller. I was lost;
> Halted without an effort to break through;
>
> (*Prelude*, VI, 592-7)

As a boy he had a memorable experience to which in after years he "oft repaired, and then would drink,/ As at a fountain," but all he can tell us about it is:

> It was, in truth,
> An ordinary sight; but I should need
> Colours and words that are unknown to man,
> To paint the visionary dreariness
> (*Prelude*, XII, 253-6)

Of another boyhood experience, he also finds little specific
to say:

> While on the perilous ridge I hung alone,
> With what strange utterance did the loud dry wind
> Blow through my ear! the sky seemed not a sky
> Of earth—and with what motion moved the clouds!
> (*Prelude*, I, 336-9)

Well, with "what strange utterance" and "what motion"?
We expect a poet to find the "language unknown to man,"
not complain about the "incompetence of human speech"
or depend upon exclamation marks. These passages, nevertheless, have power because they manage through their
intensity, through the mixture of unexpected and imaginative detail (why *dry* wind? *through* my ear? *unfathered*
vapour?) and pregnant abstractions ("visionary dreari-
ness") to communicate the sensation of the incommunicable. In his note to "The Thorn" cited above, Wordsworth
was arguing for the power of simply repeating words
and phrases, such as "Oh misery!" to project the sense of
feelings, although the "deficiencies of language" prevented
accurate analysis. *Lyrical Ballads* experimented with ways
of communicating feelings, particularly a way that uses
the lyric intensity and the narrative structure of the ballad
in order to describe people in situations that are essential
and universalizing.

Thus—to return to the passage quoted from *Tintern
Abbey*—Wordsworth's poetry of the *Lyrical Ballads* period
begins with an "I have felt," and tries to recreate that feeling
for the reader by describing it thematically and circum-
stantially. The importance is not, he insists, in the event,

which is no more than the setting or the catalyst, but in the feeling observer, who—despite the "I"—is not simply William Wordsworth, but rather observing humanity, "the mind of man." The feeling "disturbs"—that is, it moves and creates power. This is therefore what Thomas De Quincey, admittedly influenced by Wordsworth, called the "Literature of Power."[4] The whole experience leads to the "Joy/ Of elevated thoughts." Joy is pervasive in Wordsworth's *Lyrical Ballads*, as we shall see in more detail in Chapter Six. It is a profound sort of joy, so simple that it is sophisticated—often a joy of the commonplace or the pathetic. Indeed, the surface subject may not seem to be joyful at all—forsaken women, decrepit old men, idiot boys. The joy might perhaps better be called peace, the "peace that passeth understanding." It partakes of a sense of inevitability associated with the acceptance of things, coming to terms with life; it derives from the resolution of feelings into concepts which are "elevated thoughts," capable of lifting the observer-reader to the plane of the universal, creating that good feeling that accompanies a sensation of being and belonging, and is essentially a means of overcoming alienation. As Wordsworth put it in lines probably written in the spring of 1798,[5] and therefore in the *Lyrical Ballads* context:

> for in all things
> He saw one life, and felt that it was joy.
> (*The Pedlar* 217-8; cf. *The Prelude*,
> 1805, II, 429-30)

Something of the role of joy as the connecting agency between the individual and the universal is also suggested in the lines published in 1814 as part of the "Prospectus" for *The Excursion*, but possibly written as early as the spring of 1798, and certainly in the *Lyrical Ballads* ambience.[6] I quote the version of MS 1, which probably dates from 1800:

Of joy in various commonality spread;
Of the individual Mind that keeps her own
Inviolate retirement, and consists
With being limitless, the one great Life
I sing:

(18-23)

In poems written under this impulse of "commonality," the whole scene has an elemental, unitary quality which either strains out the individual and specific, or reduces them to prosaic, domesticated verisimilitude that merely authenticates the typical. All we know about Goody Blake is that she was an old woman who took a few twigs from a hedge so that she could warm herself by a fire. Behind this action is the whole drama of the Enclosure Acts that eliminated the common "wastes" from which the poor used to gather sticks to warm their hearths; she represents a type, a social problem, and is even given a characteristic name—"Goody"—which tends to convert her into everyone's grandmother. We know that the superstitious narrator of "The Thorn" has measured the "muddy pond" and found it "three feet long, and two feet wide." But this fact is presented more to qualify him as a hard-headed observer than to give the reader a localized picture. And in the passage from *Tintern Abbey* before us, the sky is just "blue"—its distinctive, universal color. The ocean is "round," surely not a visual description at all, but an intellectual one for the "mind of man." "Round" is a very physical term, but in this context it is abstracting and universalizing. "Living air" is not something observed, but something conceived and projected. It reflects a reaction of the persona, a feeling of animation. This whole description does not derive directly from the "eye upon the object,"[7] except as the object is the observer who feels and relates to the experience. Relation is characteristic of this poetry; it pulls the observer into the situation or makes him feel his way into it. As we read Wordsworth's central poems of the *Lyrical Ballads*, we are led by a special kind of universalizing description to share the experience. We have fellow feelings with Betty Foy and Simon Lee; we are both the father of the "Anecdote" and the little boy being unwittingly taught to lie; with the poet-persona we question the little girl about her dead brother and sister, and we enter into her answers. If we had to find one word as the key to these poems, perhaps it would be "empathy." But there is no need to find one word; for these poems it is better to use Wordsworth's phrase "various commonality." Wordsworth's well-known letter to John Wilson in June of 1802, mainly discussing "The Idiot Boy," is sometimes a bit pompous, but its conclusion probably gives a fairly accurate insight into the impulse behind the *Lyrical Ballads*:

This proves that the feelings there delineated (are) such as all men *may* sympathize with. This is enough for my purpose. (It) is not enough for me as a poet, to delineate merely such feelings as all men *do* sympathize with but, it is also highly desirable to add to these others, such as all men *may* sympathize with, and such as there is reason to believe they would be better and more moral beings if they did sympathize with. (*EY*, p. 358)

CHAPTER ONE

The Beginnings
of the *Lyrical Ballads*

The history of the *Lyrical Ballads* is a typically human one of false starts, mixed motivations, delays and changes of plans, accidents and cross purposes. The little volume took shape in a fortuitous way, influenced by the eagerness to serve of a pompous but kindly publisher, Joseph Cottle; by the constant financial pressures on middle-class poets, whose pride as well as their necessity made for uneasy commercial arrangements to pay the fiddler or even just buy the cheese; and by the sheer productivity of Wordsworth and Coleridge, especially the former, in the Alfoxden atmosphere.

The well-known description which Coleridge gives of the "occasion of the Lyrical Ballads" in Chapter XIV of his *Biographia Literaria* tells a fascinating and plausible tale that we must take as our starting point:

The thought suggests itself (to which of us I do not recollect) that a series of poems might be composed of two sorts. In the one, the incidents and agents were to be, in part at least, supernatural; and the excellence aimed at was to consist in the interesting of the affections by the dramatic truth of such emotions, as would naturally accompany such situations, supposing them real. And real in *this* sense they have been to every human being who, from whatever source of delusion, has at any time believed himself under supernatural agency. For the second class, subjects were to be chosen from ordinary life; the characters and incidents were to be such, as will be found in every village and its vicinity, where there is a meditative and feeling mind to seek after them, or to notice them, when they present themselves.

In this idea originated the plan of the "Lyrical Ballads"; in which it was agreed, that my endeavours should be directed to persons and characters supernatural, or at least romantic; yet so as to transfer from our inward nature a human interest and a semblance of truth sufficient to procure for these shadows of imagination that willing suspension of disbelief for the moment, which constitutes poetic faith. Mr. Wordsworth, on the other hand, was to propose to himself as his object, to give the charm of novelty to things of every day, and to excite a feeling analogous to the supernatural, by awakening the mind's attention from the lethargy of custom, and directing it to the loveliness and the wonders of the world before us; an inexhaustible treasure, but for which, in consequence of the film of familiarity and selfish solicitude we have eyes, yet see not, ears that hear not, and hearts that neither feel nor understand.

With this view I wrote "The Ancient Mariner," and was preparing among other poems, "The Dark Ladie," and the "Christabel," in which I should have more nearly realized my ideal, than I had done in my first attempt. But Mr. Wordsworth's industry proved so much more successful, and the number of his poems so much greater, that my compositions, instead of forming a balance, appeared rather an interpolation of heterogeneous matter. Mr. Wordsworth added two or three poems written in his own character, in the impassioned, lofty, and sustained diction, which is characteristic of his genius. In this form the "Lyrical Ballads" were published; and were presented by him, as an *experiment*, whether subjects, which from their nature rejected the usual ornaments and extra-colloquial style of poems in general, might not be so managed in the language of ordinary life as to produce the pleasurable interest, which it is the peculiar business of poetry to impart.

Sometimes these familiar statements are carelessly used as the basis for a description of *Lyrical Ballads* as containing two kinds of poetry—supernatural and commonplace—by Coleridge and Wordsworth respectively. Of course Coleridge does not say that: he makes a clear distinction between the volume as originally planned and as finally published, noting that Wordsworth "added two or three poems in his own character" and recognizing "The Ancient Mariner" as the sole remnant of his own intended contribution. Nevertheless, the account can be misleading about the genesis of *Lyrical Ballads*. Coleridge's version at the least greatly simplifies the matter and, as Mark Reed has well pointed out,[1] it is doubtful if such a "plan" as he described had any very solid or long-continued existence. Not only was Coleridge writing from a memory of nearly twenty years, and after an awkward estrangement had altered the relationship between the two men, but he was also producing a kind of defense of his own literary career. His version of the division of labor between the poets may even be to some extent, consciously or unconsciously, a rationale for the prominent position of his own "Ancient Mariner" and an answer to Wordsworth's ungracious comments about it in a note in the 1800 edition of *Lyrical Ballads*, and an implied criticism of Wordsworth for leaving "Christabel" out of that edition.

At any rate, there is no contemporary evidence to support Coleridge's view of the two-fold intention of the collection, unless one wishes so to interpret Wordsworth's well-known remarks in the Prologue to *Peter Bell*.[2] There he somewhat reluctantly gives up his fairy barge "like the crescent-moon," which in some sense symbolizes the supernatural, and returns prosaicaly to "the common growth of mother-earth." Part of this was written in the *Lyrical Ballads* context, and *Peter Bell* may well have begun as in some ways a "things of every day" analogue to "Ancient Mariner." However, *Peter Bell* actually contains an amalgam of superstition and the supernatural, Methodistical in flavor; and the famous "long have I loved what I behold" passage in the Prologue is an addition in MS 5[3]—closer in time to the 1819 Dedication of *Peter Bell* to Southey, and Wordsworth's effort to distinguish his more earthy imagination from Southy's supernatural epic muse, that it is to the 1798 collaboration with Coleridge.

Some twenty years later than the *Biographia Literaria*, Wordsworth makes a reference to Coleridge's account of the *Lyrical Ballads* episode in his notes for Miss Fenwick, in connection with "We Are Seven": the poets "began to talk of a Volume, which was to consist, as Mr. Coleridge has told the world, of Poems chiefly on natural subjects taken from common life, but looked at, as much as might be, through an imaginative medium" (*PW*, I, 361). But of course this is not precisely what Coleridge had told the world. It may stand as a synopsis of the poetic theory Coleridge says the two poets then shared, but Wordsworth's version of the plan of the volume is different in emphasis, and says nothing about the supernatural or any division of labor. Furthermore, Wordsworth did not in fact deny himself recourse to supernatural elements in his poems when he wanted them: witness the magic stirring of the hill of moss in "The Thorn" and Harry Gill shivering perpetually from Goody Blake's curse— events which even if they have psychological explanations depend on a belief in the supernatural. It is worth noting also that neither the Advertisement to the 1798 edition nor the Preface added to the 1800 edition says anything about any such two-pronged effort as Coleridge describes, although such an explanation *could* have been possible without disclosing the dual authorship. Their rationale for the collection is closer to that which Hazlitt says Coleridge gave him in 1798:

He said the *Lyrical Ballads* were an experiment about to be tried by him and Wordsworth, to see how far the public taste would endure poetry written in a more natural and simple style than had hitherto been attempted; totally discarding the artifices of poetical diction, and making use only of such words as had probably been common in the most ordinary language since the days of Henry II.[4]

Of course Hazlitt wrote these words many years after his meeting with the poets, and he may have been influenced by the later Advertisement or Preface—but then, he could as well have been influenced by the *Biographia Literaria* if he were padding his memory from published materials. The reference to Henry II rings true.

Coleridge's own more nearly contemporary comment talks about content rather than style, but still mentions only a one-directional experiment. Explaining to Humphry Davy on October 9, 1800, why it had been decided to leave "Christabel" out of the second edition of *Lyrical Ballads*, he says the chief reason was that "the poem was in direct opposition to the very purpose for which the Lyrical Ballads were published—viz—an experiment to see how far those passions, which alone give any value to extraordinary Incidents, were capable of interesting, in & for themselves, in the incidents of common Life" (*Letters*, I, 631). The language of Coleridge's point sounds more like the Preface, which Wordsworth had just written, than the 1798 Advertisement, which has the same stylistic emphasis as Hazlitt's memory of Coleridge's 1798 version of the experiment. Unless he is making a distinction between planned and published, he appears to be contradicting his *Biographia Literaria* statement which claims that "Ancient Mariner" and "Christabel" were designed to fulfill his part of the collaboration. Of course it is possible that Coleridge's explanation to Davy is all a rationalization, that for complicated reasons he had not finished "Christabel." But on the surface Wordsworth made a decision for reasons Coleridge is presenting, and these indicate that at least by 1800 Wordsworth did not have or was not supposed to have any notion of a dual purpose in *Lyrical Ballads.*

The "Ancient Mariner" does seem to have been the nucleus around which the *Lyrical Ballads* grew, although probably in a much less systematic fashion than the two authors' later accounts suggest. Wordsworth says in his remarks to Miss Fenwick that "in the spring of the year 1798" he, Coleridge, and Dorothy walked from Alfoxden towards Watchet, intending a visit to the "Valley of Stones," and agreed to defray their expenses by writing a poem to be published in the *Monthly Magazine*. With this modest aim and no more than five Pounds in view, they "planned the Poem of The Ancient Mariner." However, since the poem "grew and grew till it became too important" for that purpose, they "began to talk of a Volume" of imaginative treatments of natural subjects, and Wordsworth says he "accordingly . . . wrote The Idiot Boy, Her eyes are wild, etc., We Are Seven, The Thorn and some others" (*PW*, I, 361). Coleridge confirms this famous walk in a note—first published in *Sibylline Leaves* in 1817—to the first stanza of Part IV on "The Ancient Mariner," in which he acknowledges his indebtedness to Wordsworth for having given him the last two lines of the stanza:

> And thou art long, and lank, and brown,
> As is the ribbed sea-sand

and continues, "It was on a delightful walk from Nether Stowey to Dulverton, with him and his sister, in the Autumn of 1797, that this Poem was planned, and in part composed."

Coleridge's memory is more accurate than Wordsworth's on the time: it was in the "Autumn of 1797," as a letter of Dorothy's, probably to Mary Hutchinson, on November 20, 1797, makes clear:

We have been on another tour: we set off last Monday evening at half past four. The evening was dark and cloudy: we went eight miles, William and Coleridge employing themselves in laying the plan of a ballad, to be published with some pieces of William's.[5]

"Last Monday" of the fateful trip was November 13, and "another tour" probably refers back to a trip which

Dorothy describes in an earlier letter. That time they went through Porlock and close to the sea to Lynmouth, Devonshire, where the next morning they "were guided to a valley at the top of one of those immense hills which open at each end to the sea, and is from its rocky appearance called the Valley of Stones" (*EY*, p. 194)—the modern Valley of Rocks, a mile or so west of Lynton—and then apparently came back across Exmore to Dulverton. Possibly Wordsworth confused the two journeys as well as the date in his recollection for Miss Fenwick. The important point, on which all evidence seems to agree, is that a volume, including "some pieces of William's" was projected, and that it grew out of a cooperative effort by Wordsworth and Coleridge to write a poem together.

That the impulse to such joint composition was most probably Coleridge's is evident from a note he supplied in 1828 to the fragment of a prose poem, "The Wanderings of Cain," which he says "was written in the year 1798, near Nether Stowey" and was to have been composed "in concert with another, whose name is too venerable within the precincts of genius to be unnecessarily brought into connection with such a trifle, and who was then residing at a small distance from Nether Stowey." Obviously this venerated neighbor was Wordsworth and, according to Coleridge's note, the two were in one night to write a three-canto work, following a scheme drawn up by Coleridge. Wordsworth was to have done the first canto, Coleridge the second, and whoever finished first the third:

Almost thirty years have passed by; yet at this moment I cannot without something more than a smile moot the question which of the two things was the more impracticable, for a mind so eminently original to compose another man's thoughts and fancies, or for a taste so austerely pure and simple to imitate the Death of Abel? Methinks I see his grand and noble countenance as at the moment when having dispatched my own portion of the task at full fingerspeed, I hastened to him with my manuscript —that look of humorous despondency fixed on his almost blank sheet of paper, and then its silent mock-piteous admission of failure struggling with the sense of the exceeding ridiculousness of the whole scheme—which broke up in a laugh: and the Ancient Mariner was written instead.

If the "Ancient Mariner" was indeed written "instead," then Coleridge's date is wrong on this note, and the Cain episode must have happened sooner, possibly on the earlier visit to the Valley of Rocks which Dorothy recorded. Apparently the spot was a favorite one with the Nether Stowey group, for in April 1798 Coleridge urged Cottle to come and "go on a roam to Linton and Linmouth" and "the vast valley of stones" (Letters, I, 403)—a trip which the publisher's reminiscences later recorded; and when Hazlitt came to visit in late May, Coleridge and John Chester took him, as Hazlitt describes in his essay "First Acquaintance with Poets," on the same route "through Minehead and by the Blue Anchor, and on to Linton" (Howe, XVII, 119). In the Valley of Rocks (which Hazlitt wrongly suspected of being "only the poetical name for it,") Coleridge reported that "he and Wordsworth were to have made this place the scene of a prose-tale, which was to have been in the manner of, but far superior to, the Death of Abel, but they relinquished the design" (Howe, XVII, 120).

Whatever the dating, here is further evidence of Coleridge's trying to get Wordsworth involved in a joint project, and all the designs turn out to be relinquished or modified. According to his own account to Miss Fenwick, Wordsworth entered fully into the notion of writing "The Ancient Mariner" with Coleridge; and although he modestly says "much the greatest part of the story was Mr. Coleridge's invention," he still claims credit for suggesting "certain parts" of the plot. He had just been reading Shelvock's Voyages and proposed that the hero be represented as having killed an albatross and be pursued by avenging tutelary spirits. He also contributed the notion of the ship's being navigated by dead men, and says he furnished "two or three lines at the beginning of the poem, in particular":

> And listened like a three years child;
> The Mariner had his will.

The sequel, however, is very much like that which Coleridge records for "The Wanderings of Cain":

As we endeavored to proceed conjointly (I speak of the same evening) our respective manners proved so widely different that it would have been quite presumptuous in me to do anything but separate from an undertaking upon which I could only have been a clog. (*PW*, I, 361)

The effort to collaborate on the same poem seems to have lasted only one "memorable evening"—as Wordsworth called it. Since he supplied the core of the plot of "The Ancient Mariner," and the lines which he claims and those Coleridge attributes to him have the authentic magic, the reason he felt the two poets' respective manners differed fatally is not immediately clear—especially how the unbridgeable difference could have been suddenly discovered in one night. Possibly there is some hint in Coleridge's complaint to Hazlitt, that May of 1798, that Wordsworth "was not prone enough to believe in the traditional superstitions of the place, and that there was a something corporeal, a *matter-of-factness*, a clinging to the palpable, or often to the petty, in his poetry" (Howe, XVII, 117). It may be significant that Wordsworth later objected to the archaisms in the poem, which was first called "The Rime of the Ancyent Marinere";[6] perhaps this is at least part of what he could not adjust to.

Then the difference between Wordsworth and Coleridge may have been in their philosophical and moral attitudes toward the story—not in its palpability, but in its humanity. Coleridge was at the time much the more doctrinaire of the two in Christian belief. He was then even preaching occasionally at Unitarian congregations—Hazlitt walked

ten miles in the mud to hear him preach in January 1798,
and was as "delighted" as if he "had heard the music of
the spheres." (Lamb later and more irreverently responded
to Coleridge's question whether he had ever heard him
preach: "I never heard you do anything else.") Only the
opportune gift of an annuity from the Wedgewood brothers kept Coleridge from accepting a call from a Unitarian
congregation in early 1798. He wrote the Reverend John
Estlin on May 18 of that year, that he and Wordsworth
could not even discuss religion: "On one subject we are
habitually silent—we found our date dissimilar, & never
renewed the subject. . . . he loves & venerates Christ &
Christianity—I wish, he did more" (*Letters*, I, 410). Wordsworth may not have been able to go all the way with the
attitude expressed in the conclusion:

> He prayeth best, who loveth best
> All things both great and small;
> For the dear God who loveth us,
> He made and loveth all.
>
> (614-17)

The sentiments, however, do not seem foreign to Wordsworth's views as reflected in *Peter Bell* and the "sense of
Being" passages in *The Prelude*,[7] and it may be that the
difficulty in collaboration was not so much religious
as moral: Coleridge's approach to the subject—say especially the fate of the Pilot's boy—may have seemed to
Wordsworth too implacable in its morality. It may be
relevant that he later objected to Barron Field about
Coleridge's treatment of similar material in "The Three
Graves": "I gave him the subject"—discovery of the manuscripts now reveals that Wordsworth actually wrote the
first two books of the poem—"but he made it too shocking
and painful, and not sufficiently sweetened by any healing
views."[8]

Still another possibility is that the difference in "respective manners" of the two poets was in facility and address

to composition. Wordsworth wrote his friend William
Matthews at the end of 1794 that he had neither "quickness
of penmanship, nor rapidity of composition" (*EY*, p. 137)
—and though he developed facility, his composition was
characteristically labored. We remember the speed with
which Coleridge reports that he finished his part of the
"Wanderings of Cain" assignment; and there is the comment, amusing enough in the light of Coleridge's own
procrastination and dilatoriness, in his letter to Davy on
July 25, 1800, about the problems of the second edition of
Lyrical Ballads: "W. Wordsworth is such a lazy fellow that
I bemire myself by making promises for him" (*Letters*,
I, 611). Certainly some complacent criticism is implied in
Coleridge's telling Hazlitt that he "liked to compose in
walking over uneven ground" whereas Wordsworth "always wrote (if he could) walking up and down a straight
gravel-walk, or in some spot where the continuity of his
verse met with no collateral interruption" (Howe, XVII,
119).

And finally, Wordsworth may simply have found it
impossible to write a poem jointly, any poem, with
Coleridge or anybody else. What we know of the independence of Wordsworth's character makes it curious that
he should have seriously contemplated such a project.
Only the force of Coleridge's urgings could have accounted
for it. True, Wordsworth was going to collaborate with
William Matthews in publishing *The Philanthropist*, but
that was Matthew's proposal, Wordsworth made many
conditions, and nothing ever came of it. He also was
working with Francis Wrangham in 1795 on an Imitation of
Juvenal, but this project too was still-born, and in 1806
Wordsworth was a little sharp in denying Wrangham's
efforts to resuscitate it.[9] Wordsworth was not a collab-
orator. He was glad to have help of various kinds—he
could call upon Davy or De Quincey to see his works
through the press, or eagerly hope that Coleridge's conversation could somehow bring off the great philosophical

poem that Coleridge was convinced his friend could write and "do great good." But even this was Coleridge's idea, and we suspect that the whole notion of *Lyrical Ballads* as a joint effort came from him also.

As we piece the story together, we conclude that Coleridge liked the idea of some joint publication, Wordsworth was simply dedicated to writing poetry, and that the project that started from "The Ancient Mariner" and became the *Lyrical Ballads* did not for a time have a predominant position in their fluctuating plans. In fact, despite Wordsworth's later memory of talking of a "volume" to grow out of "Ancient Mariner," and Dorothy's contemporary indication of a plan to publish the ballad with a few poems of her brother's, Coleridge was for a time still toying with bringing out the poem by himself. Early in January 1798, when Coleridge was "utterly without money" and desperately trying to scrounge together enough to pay off some eighteen Pounds of debts, he wrote John Estlin asking for a loan of ten Pounds, and proposing to "sell my Ballad to Phillips who I doubt not will give me 5£ for it" (*Letters*, I, 368). This is the original plan to publish the poem in the *Monthly Magazine*, of which Richard Phillips was the proprietor—a plan which the Wordsworths thought had been abandoned, and which Coleridge may have retrieved only momentarily to show Estlin that he was trying to do something himself to solve his financial problems.

Nevertheless, on February 18 Coleridge wrote Joseph Cottle: "I have finished my ballad—it is 340 lines. I am going on with the Visions—all together (for I shall print two scenes of my Tragedy, as fragments) I can add 1500 lines—Now what do you advise?—Shall I add my Tragedy, & so make a second Volume—? or pursue my first intention of inserting the 1500 lines in the 3rd Edition?" (*Letters*, I, 387).

Here is no suggestion of any joint publication with Wordsworth. Coleridge is asking Cottle whether the "Ancient Mariner"—assuming, as seems most likely, that was his "ballad"—should be put along with his *Destiny of Nations* and fragments from his tragedy to add 1500 lines for the third edition of *Poems on Various Subjects* (1796, 1797), or whether the new poems should be published separately or with the whole of *Osorio* in a second volume. Actually, the third edition did not develop until 1803; and the tragedy, revised as *Remorse*, was not published until 1813. Coleridge's problem in early 1798 was that although the Wedgewoods had just offered him an annuity of £150 nothing had yet been paid, and his situation was desperate: "my money is utterly expended." Estlin had responded generously to Coleridge's January petition—providing fifteen guineas—and possibly forestalling "The Ancient Mariner" 's being sent off to the *Monthly Magazine*—but Coleridge still owed at least £10 of that £18, five guineas of it being his mother-in-law's quarterly allowance, which lay "heavily" upon him. These February proposals to Cottle were probably top-of-the-head suggestions, designed to get an advance from the publisher, but they demonstrate how uncommitted Coleridge was at the time to the grand scheme he later describes in *Biographia Literaria*.

Meanwhile, Wordsworth was keeping several poetic balls uncertainly in the air. When Coleridge first came to visit Dorothy and William at Racedown in June 1797, the sister wrote to "a friend"—probably Mary Hutchinson— about the activities of the two poets: "The first thing that was read after he came was William's new poem *The Ruined Cottage* with which he was much delighted; and after tea he repeated to us two acts and a half of his tragedy *Osorio*. The next morning William read his tragedy *The Borderers*."[10] These works reflect the two main areas of Wordsworth's poetic projects at the time: the play and serious blank verse.

In the same letter in which Dorothy announced the plan of publishing a ballad "with some pieces of William's," she noted: "William's play is finished, and sent to the managers of the Covent Garden Theater. We have not the faintest expectation that it will be accepted" (*EY*, p. 194). So they told themselves, but by December 8, 1797, Dorothy was writing her brother Christopher at Trinity College, Cambridge, that they had been in London for more than a week because Wordsworth had "been induced to come up to alter his play for the stage at the suggestion of one of the principal actors." On December 13, however, Wordsworth was telling Cottle disappointedly that his play was rejected and they would stop by Bristol on their way back to Alfoxden. So much for the tragedy. On March 6 Wordsworth assured his friend James Tobin that if he ever again tried a play he would make it either a closet drama or a stage piece—"There is no middle way." But he had no expectation of working on a play or anything else, apparently, except his long philosophical poem:

I have written 1300 lines of a poem in which I contrive to convey most of the knowledge of which I am possessed. My object is to give pictures of Nature, Man, and Society. Indeed I know not any thing which will not come within the scope of my plan. . . . But the work of composition is carved out for me, for at least a year and a half to come. The essays of which I have spoken to you must be written with eloquence, or not at all. My eloquence, speaking with modesty, will all be carried off, at least for some time, into my poem. (*EY*, p. 212)

Five days later he wrote similarly to James Losh: "I have written 1300 lines of a poem which I hope to make of considerable utility; its title will be *The Recluse or views of Nature, Man, and Society*" (*EY*, p. 214). Coleridge encouraged *this* activity, as is evident from a letter of March 7 to Cottle about "The Giant Wordsworth . . . he has written over 1200 lines of blank verse, superior, I hesitate not to aver, to anything in our language which anyway resembles it" (*Letters*, I, 391). In early March, then, Wordsworth's work was cut out for at least a year and a half on this solemn duty—he says nothing about any short pieces such as were to make up the *Lyrical Ballads*.

Coleridge, however, was still pushing for some kind of joint publishing effort. About March 13, 1798, he wrote to Cottle a curious letter—curious in the light of the supposed plans for publishing the ballad and a few pieces:

I am requested by Wordsworth to put the following questions— What *could* you conveniently & *prudently*, and what *would* you, give for

1   Our two Tragedies—with small prefaces containing an analysis of our principal characters. Exclusive of the prefaces, the Tragedies are together 5000 lines—which *in the printing* from the dialogue form & directions respecting actors & scenery is at least equal to 6000.—To be delivered to you within a week of the date of your answer to this letter—& the money, which you offer, to be payed to us at the end of four months from the same date—none to be payed before—all to be payed then.—

2   Wordsworth's Salisbury Plain & Tale of a Woman which two poems with a few others which he will add & the notes will make a volume (of . . . pages. *inked out in manuscript*) This to be delivered to you within 3 weeks of the date of your answer—& the money to be payed, as before, at the end of four months from the same date.— (*Letters*, I, 399-400)

There is no place here for the Valley of Rocks project, unless it can be fit somehow into the "few others" which Wordsworth would add to *Salisbury Plain*—a part of which was indeed published in *Lyrical Ballads* as "The Female Vagrant"— and the "Tale of a Woman" (which is probably "The Ruined Cottage," later to become the first book of *The Excursion*).

It appears from all this that though the friends began to "talk of a volume" in November, the idea had no priority but rather jostled with other schemes, of which Coleridge especially was fertile.

We can understand why Coleridge told Cottle he had been "requested by Wordsworth" to make the publishing proposal, since most of the material was to come from Wordsworth, but we wonder about the real source of the proposition, especially in view of the older poet's comment only about a week earlier to James Tobin: "There is little need to advise me against publishing; it is a thing which I dread as much as death itself. This may serve as an example of the figure by rhetoricians called hyperbole, but privacy and quiet are my delight."[11] Cottle reported later that Wordsworth expressed to him about this time "a strong objection" to the idea of publishing.[12] We remember that Wordsworth had not published anything—although he had considered it—since *Descriptive Sketches* in 1793, whereas Coleridge had been more recently at the presses. His *Poems on various Subjects* had been published by Cottle in 1796 and a new edition the following year, and in 1798 Coleridge brought out *Fears in Solitude . . . To which are added France, an Ode; and Frost at Midnight.* More likely Wordsworth acquiesced for financial reasons in Coleridge's suggestion that they query Cottle as to what he *could* give for the two volumes.

Such was the repeated pattern of Wordsworth's poetic career. In 1842 when it was drawing to an end, he wrote Aubrey de Vere, "Publication was ever to me most irksome; so that if I had been rich, I question whether I should ever have published at all" (*LY*, III, 1387). He was rather proud of his tragedy; he became quite agitated in early 1799 when he feared the manuscript he had left with his brother Richard before he went to Germany might have been lost, since he had no other copy. But he did not publish it until 1842. "Salisbury Plain" he had been toying with bringing out, if he would make any money on it, since 1794, when on May 23 he wrote to William Matthews: "I have another poem written last summer ready for the press, though I certainly should not publish it unless I hoped to derive from it some pecuniary recompence." By November 20, 1795, he was still saying he "should wish to dispose of" the poem if he "could get anything for it."[13] He had been making substantial alterations, however, and promised Cottle a manuscript copy of the current version in January 1796, which he duly sent him by the Pinneys in early March, when Dorothy announced to her friend Jane Marshall, "Wm. is going to publish a poem." Just when and why he got the manuscript back is not clear, but by May 9, 1798, the poem was not only still unpublished, but not even completed! He was writing Cottle, "I say nothing of the Salisbury plain 'till I see you, I am determined to finish it, and equally so that You shall publish. I have lately been busy about another plan which I do not wish to mention till I see you."[14] The poem went through much more tinkering —on February 27, 1799, Wordsworth wrote to Coleridge in Germany, "I also took courage to devote two days (O Wonder) to the Salisbury Plain" and told of plans to "invent a new story." Except for the "Female Vagrant" section published in *Lyrical Ballads*, "Salisbury Plain" did not see print until 1842, when it appeared as *Guilt and Sorrow*.

Therefore this two-volume proposal of Coleridge's March 13 letter did not turn out to be a viable one, for a number of reasons. Cottle's response to the proposal seems not to have survived. In his *Early Recollections: Chiefly Relating to the late Samuel Taylor Coleridge*, which was not published until 1837 and is full of inaccuracies, he claims to have offered the poets thirty guineas each for the tragedies: "which, after some hesitation, was declined, from the hope of introducing one, or both, on the stage. The volume of Poems was left for some future arrangement."[15] It appears, however, from Coleridge's letter to Cottle of April or May[16] that the publisher found himself unable "prudently" to provide what the poets expected, and possibly offered less than they thought their

dramas were worth. Coleridge emphasizes that he strained
for six or seven months on *Osorio* and Wordsworth put
even more time and genius into *The Borderers.* They did
not, he explains, really want to publish their plays, still
hoping that happier times might see them produced at
greater profits (Wordsworth had been much impressed by
Monk Lewis' bonanza from *The Castle Spectre*)—but "our
thoughts were bent on a plan for the accomplishment of
which, a certain sum of money was necessary, (the whole)
at that particular time, and in order to this we resolved,
although reluctantly, to part with our Tragedies"— provided they could get thirty guineas apiece for them. Now,
however, they had decided not to publish the plays in any
event, but to seek other means of getting the desired funds.
Cottle may still have Wordsworth's "volume of Poems" if
he wishes "at the price mentioned, to be paid at the time
specified, *i.e.* thirty guineas, to be paid sometime in the last
fortnight of July." This "volume of Poems" is presumably
the same "Salisbury Plain & Tale of a Woman with a few
others." At any rate, they are clearly Wordsworth's poems:
still nothing is hinted about "The Ancient Mariner" or any
collaboration with Coleridge.

Possibly other negotiations intervened between this letter (*Letters,,* I, 402) and the one asking what Cottle could
prudently offer (*Letters,* I, 399-400), because no price was
there mentioned. It is even possible that Cottle, despite his
later memories of wishful projections, actually offered
twenty guineas apiece for the tragedies—justifying Coleridge's anger—to be paid by the desired date, and held
forth vague future rewards for the volume of Wordsworth's poems, depending upon the length and possible
sale. Dorothy was later under the impression that for
Lyrical Ballads Wordsworth was to receive "a certain
present price and is to be paid afterwards in proportion to
their sale." It seems likely that Cottle had made some
proposals in April which Dorothy at least thought had been

accepted, because she wrote brother Richard on April 30
that William was "about to publish some poems. He is to
have twenty guineas for one volume, and he expects more
than twice as much for another which is nearly ready for
publishing."[17] Loyal Dorothy was always trying to put the
best front on William's practical, money-earning sagacity
in her communications with their elder brother, a hard-
headed lawyer, and she would not necessarily have told
him that Coleridge was to provide half of the first volume;
but such a situation might account for the second one
producing twice as much return. If Dorothy is not talking
about the project combining the tragedies, "Salisbury
Plain," and "Tale of a Woman," possibly there was still
another publishing plan before the two poets were to get
back to the *Lyrical Ballads*.

Coleridge told Cottle on about May 28 that Wordsworth
"would not object to the publishing of Peter Bell *or* the
Salisbury Plain, singly; but to the publishing of *his poems*
in two volumes he is decisively repugnant & oppugnant."
Possibly, as Mrs. Moorman has suggested (I, 372), at one
point Cottle had offered to publish two volumes of Wordsworth's poems, one containing "Salisbury Plain" and *Peter
Bell*, the other shorter verses. Or possibly the first volume
Dorothy spoke of was what turned out to be the *Lyrical
Ballads*, and she halved the return since Coleridge was
contributing to that also. In fact, according to Dorothy
(*EY*, 227) Cottle finally offered Wordsworth thirty guineas
for his part in that volume, roughly two-thirds of the
whole.

It seems more likely, however, that on April 30 the only
publishing project upon which Cottle had yet made an offer
was a "Salisbury Plain" package; because, as we remember, on May 9 Wordsworth was promising to talk with
Cottle about that poem when they met, but had been
"busy about another plan" which he wanted to discuss
with the publisher. This "another plan," I think, was the

final fruition of the first volume of the *Lyrical Ballads*.
Cottle played his part in being available and eager to help.

In his first surviving letter to Cottle, probably January
1797, Wordsworth thanked the Bristol bookseller and
benefactor of Coleridge and Southey for sending him a
copy of Southey's *Joan of Arc*, promised to forward a
manuscript of "Salisbury Plain," and signed himself "your
very obliged friend." Generous, kindly, wooly-headed
Cottle was very obviously adding to his list of promising
young poets. He was a poet of sorts himself: early in 1798
he published *Malvern Hills*, a topographical poem with
some liberal political sentiments, a copy of which somehow
found its way to Alfoxden and, according to Dorothy,
was sent back to Bristol by coach. The poem went though
four editions; Cottle's later *Alfred*, an epic poem in twenty-
four books, saw five editions. More important, Cottle
considered himself a patron of poets. He is pompous,
complacent, and inaccurate in his recollections about
Wordsworth, but nonetheless has some justifications for
his pride:

A visit to Mr. Coleridge at Stowey, had been the means of my
introduction to Mr. Wordsworth, who read me many of his
Lyrical Pieces, when I perceived in them, a peculiar, but decided
merit. I advised him to publish them, expressing a belief that
they would be well received. I further said that he should be at
no risk; that I would give him the same sum which I had given
Mr. Coleridge and Mr. Southey, and that it would be a gratifying
circumstance to me, to usher into the world, by becoming the
publisher of the first volumes of three such Poets, as Southey,
Coleridge, and Wordsworth; a distinction that might never again
occur to a Provincial bookseller.
To the idea of publishing he expressed a strong objection, and
after several interviews, I left him, with an earnest wish that he
would reconsider his determination (*Early Recollections*, I, 309).

There are obvious errors in this account: Cottle probably
met Wordsworth before the Stowey period—he apparently

sent the *Joan of Arc* to him at Racedown—and he could not have been his first publisher, since Johnson had brought out *An Evening Walk* and *Descriptive Sketches*; but Cottle's achievement was nevertheless remarkable indeed for a provincial bookseller. And he kept at it until he did "usher in" the *Lyrical Ballads* after a fashion, although he left it to shift for itself with unseemly haste. He persistently offered various services to Wordsworth and Coleridge. On August 18, 1797, William thanked him for two guineas and gratefully declined a draft which assistance from Thomas Poole had made unnecessary. Again on September 13 Wordsworth expressed his appreciation of offers of "pecuniary accommodation" not required at the moment, but by February or March 1798 he was glad to accept ten Pounds, and also asked that Cottle contrive to borrow for him a copy of Erasmus Darwin's *Zoonomia*.[18]

This sort of kindly pressure from a good-hearted publisher, in consort with Wordsworth's financial difficulties, was calculated to break down what scruples Wordsworth had against publishing his poems. Probably the final appearance of the *Lyrical Ballads* owed a great deal to the fact that the Wordsworths needed money just then. Because their paternal inheritance was being kept from them by the unscrupulous Lord Lowther (and was not paid until a settlement was made with the next Earl in 1803), they were largely dependent upon the 900 Pounds Raisley Calvert had left Wordsworth in 1795 in recognition, as the poet later explained to Sir George Beaumont, that he "had powers and attainments which might be of use to mankind" (*EY*, p. 546). The moral obligation of such a gift, as much as Coleridge's urging and confidence in his own powers, helped to focus Wordsworth's attention on the serious *Recluse* rather than on short poems of the *Lyrical Ballads* sort.

But although the Wordsworths had some capital and some prospects, they lacked ready cash. William wrote brother Richard on May 7, 1797, concerning his embarrassment that he could see no way of meeting the just request of his cousin Robinson for repayment of 250 Pounds which had been advanced for William's education. He had been disappointed in his settlements from the Calvert bequest, and his income was much lower than he had expected; besides, everything was "very dear for housekeeping . . . no meat under 6d," and tea and sugar, their only luxuries, were going up (*EY*, p. 184). This was at Racedown where the Pinneys were letting them live free. By next May Wordsworth had received only £30 more from the Calvert estate, and his expenses were higher at Alfoxden, where he had to pay an annual rent of £23. Out of the money that had been paid of his inheritance, Wordsworth had rashly and greedily lent £500 to Basil Montagu and Charles Douglas at 10 per cent interest—a usurious rate which he amusingly came to fear might invalidate the bills. At best this "investment" gave him an income of £50 a year. Part of this debt, £200 lent to Douglas on a note signed by Montagu and Douglas, was due on January 1, 1797; but Douglas paid only £100, and that to Montagu, who was having financial troubles of his own.[19] He may have managed to pay the interest up until November 1, 1797; but according to Dorothy's letter to her "Aunt" Rawson on July 3, 1798, Montagu had not recently been able to pay them even for looking after his son, little Basil, who had been living with the Wordsworths since late 1795. William's account to his brother Richard on February 23, 1803, makes clear that Montagu then still owed £454 although he had been making payments for the last three years, including £50 "arrears." Although in 1798 Dorothy bragged to her aunt that she and her brother had lived on their income, she listed expenses of £110 and justified the forthcoming trip to Germany by explaining that living costs would be cheaper there, they hoped to earn something from translation, and William had sold some poems.[20]

Financing that trip to Germany may have been the final spur to action on the publishing plans which had been bandied about by the Wordsworths and Coleridge, and the nudge that would bring the little book of *Lyrical Ballads* into reality. For although Dorothy extolled the practical economy of the move, there was the problem of some twenty-five guineas for transportation costs. What made the trip possible was the generosity of Thomas and Josiah Wedgewood: besides their £150 annuity to Coleridge, they ultimately loaned Wordsworth £110 to defray the expenses of the poet and his sister also (Moorman, I, 409). Such, however, had not been the Wordsworths' intention: Dorothy proudly—and as it turned out with false confidence—told her aunt: "we shall receive, before our departure much more than sufficient to defray the expenses of our journey, from a bookseller to whom William has sold some poems that are now printing" (*EY*, p. 224).

What brought the whole matter to a head was that just at the time that Coleridge miraculously had the funds to realize such a scheme as a trip to Germany, the Wordsworth's had no place to live and were ripe for an expedition. They could not renew the lease on Alfoxden—Wordsworth later said he did not try, but Coleridge and Poole were trying for him. The trouble was that the neighbors had been stirred up by the strange carryings on of the man who had no wife with him "but only a woman who passes for his Sister,"[21] who was frequently up on the heights at all times of the day and night, who asked questions about the navigability of the brook and even followed it up to its source (working on a suggestion of Coleridge for a poem on "The Brook")—and who, to top it off, was visited by the notorious radical, John Thelwall. Suspicions about this "emigrant family" reported to the Home Office actually brought down an agent to investigate, as Coleridge describes amusingly in his *Biographia Literaria* (Chap. X). Although the government took no

action, not surprisingly Mrs. St. Albyn came to consider
the Wordsworths undesirable tenants. This fact seems to
have become clear in early March. On March 5 Dorothy
wrote Mary Hutchinson: "It is decided that we quit Allfoxden—The house is left." The next day William gave Tobin
the same information, adding, "What may be our destina-
tion I cannot say." At that time Dorothy thought they
might go back to Racedown, but on March 11 William told
James Losh of a "delightful scheme"—they had "come to a
resolution" to go to Germany.[22]

The decision must have been made suddenly and spurred
the poets to action. For it was within a few days that
Coleridge wrote Cottle of a "plan" which required money
in about four months, and for which they would be willing
to publish even their tragedies. And it seems to have been
in March that William suddenly became active in writing
short lyric poems, when Dorothy told Mary (March 5),
"his faculties seem to expand every day, he composes with
more facility than he did, as to the *mechanism* of poetry,
and his ideas flow faster than he can express them"
(*EY*, p. 200).

CHAPTER TWO

The Appearance
of the *Lyrical Ballads*

Wordsworth's nineteen poems published in the first edition of *Lyrical Ballads* fall into three groups: (I) those composed before March 1798, which were apparently available for publication as the "few other poems" mentioned for inclusion in the various schemes of Coleridge and Wordsworth; (II) those written from late May to early July, when the *Lyrical Ballads* plan had already become an in-the-press reality; and in between, (III) those written from early March to mid-May, under the impulse of a special effort to produce poems for a volume to bring in money for the German expedition. The first group go back as far as 1787 and, although partly revised for the *Lyrical Ballads* publication, are not really the product of the *Lyrical Ballads* idea. The second group of poems contains partly afterthoughts which, although conceived in the *Lyrical Ballads* atmosphere, begin to suggest some of the movements away from the notion of the "experiment." These three groups are as follows:[1]

Group I

1. "Lines Left upon a Seat in a Yew-tree." Wordsworth said it was "composed in part at school at Hawkshead"

33

(1787), but most of it was probably written between February 8 and July of 1797.

2. "Lines Written near Richmond, upon the Thames, at Evening." Wordsworth said he actually observed the phenomena on the Cam, and the poem goes back to a sonnet written possibly between late 1788 and 1791. A version called "Written on the Thames near Richmond" is dated March 29, 1797. The final version was probably written sometime between that date and May 30, 1798.

3. "The Female Vagrant." Possibly composed in some form about 1791, incorporated in "Salisbury Plain," probably by late 1793.

4. "The Convict." Written in 1796, probably between March 21 and early October.

5. "Old Man Travelling." Begun as "Description of a Beggar," probably late 1796 or early 1797.

Group II

1. "Expostulation and Reply." Probably composed between May 23 and June 12, 1798.

2. "The Tables Turned." Composed at the same time as "Expostulation and Reply."

3. "Lines Composed a Few Miles above Tintern Abbey." Written between July 10 and 13, 1798.

Group III

1. "Lines written at a small distance from my House, and sent by my little Boy to the Person to whom they are addressed" (later "To My Sister"). Written between March 1 and 9, 1798, probably March 6-9.

(Numbers 2 through 8 written between early March and about May 16, 1798.)

2. "Goody Blake and Harry Gill"

3. "Simon Lee"

4. "We Are Seven"
5. "The Last of the Flock"
6. "The Mad Mother"
7. "The Idiot Boy"
8. "Complaint of a Forsaken Indian Woman"
9. "The Thorn." Begun March 19, and probably composed soon thereafter, certainly by about May 16.
(Numbers 10 and 11 composed between early March or, more probably, early April and about May 16, 1798.)
10. "Anecdote for Fathers"
11. "Lines Written in Early Spring"

The eleven poems in this last group are probably the *pièce de resistance* of the *Lyrical Ballads* as Wordsworth conceived it, the core of the "experiment," for which the Advertisement and later the Preface were written. Some of these are probably what Wordsworth had in mind when he wrote Cottle on April 12, "You will be pleased to hear that I have gone on very rapidly adding to my stock of poetry"—a curiously mercantile figure, but perhaps appropriate enough for an author to a publisher. It was probably most of these poems which Dorothy referred to in her letter to Richard of April 30 as intended to make up a volume "nearly ready for publishing."[2] That elusive volume was to take still more doing, but Wordsworth was working at it with a new energy.

Dorothy's *Journal* for March 23 records a significant and perhaps catalytic event: "Coleridge dined with us. He brought his ballad finished. We walked with him to the Miner's house. A beautiful evening, very starry, the horned moon." Who can doubt that they read the poem, and Dorothy was struck by its description of

> The horned Moon, with one bright Star
> Almost atween the tips
>
> (1798 *version*, 201-2)?

The poem which started on the Valley of Rocks expedition as a collaborative effort was finally "finished." Coleridge had announced his "ballad" finished once before, on February 18, but with 340 lines: the published version of "The Ancient Mariner" has 658. If the "ballad" completed earlier was "The Ancient Mariner"—as seems most likely, since of the other possible candidates, there is no evidence that "The Dark Ladie" was ever so long, or that Coleridge could have thought it or "Christabel" completed then— "The Ancient Mariner" grew considerably.[3]

Possibly the additions to "Ancient Mariner" were in the area of enlarging the supernatural aspects. Wordsworth's remarks on his memory of the original scheme make no mention of many features such as the spectre ship and the dice game between Death and Death-in-Life. Meanwhile, as we have seen, Wordsworth had at least started "The Thorn," which he said in an 1800 note to *Lyrical Ballads* was designed "to exhibit some of the general laws by which superstition acts upon the mind." In late February or early March, we remember, William wrote Cottle asking him urgently to borrow a copy of Erasmus Darwin's *Zoonomia* and send it *"by the first carrier."* About March 13, Dorothy thanked Cottle for the books: "They have already completely answered the purpose for which William wrote for them."[4] Probably Wordsworth's purpose was to verify the story of Goody Blake and Harry Gill. He told Miss Fenwick, "The incident from Dr. Darwin's *Zoonomia*"; this is certainly a tale which also treats the "laws by which superstition acts upon the mind." On April 20 Dorothy's *Journal* notes, *"Peter Bell* begun"—another poem which fits into the same category.

All through this March, Dorothy complained to her *Journal* about the cold bleak weather and the slowly advancing spring, until suddenly on Easter Sunday, April 8, the air was "oppressively warm." Mrs. Moorman (I, 389) calls attention to the parallel of Coleridge's lines in Part IV of "The Three Graves":

> 'Twas such a foggy time as makes
> Old Sextons, Sir! like me,
> Rest on their spades to cough; the spring
> Was late uncommonly.
>
> And then the hot days, all at once,
> They came we knew not how:
> You looked about for shade, when scarce
> A leaf was on a bough.
>
> (468-75)

Possibly these verses were written that April, as Coleridge took up again "The Three Graves," a poem which apparently Wordsworth began, wrote part of (certainly Book II and presumably Book I), and then turned over to Coleridge, who wrote Books III and IV in 1797-1798. All four of these pieces ("The Thorn," "Goody Blake," "The Three Graves" and *Peter Bell*) have the supernatural in the background, but implicitly or explicitly offer psychological and physical explanations for the phenomena; *Peter Bell* does so most explicitly. They suggest an analogue to Coleridge's verses making the supernatural appear real: "And real in *this* sense they have been to every human being who, from whatever species of delusion, has at any time believed himself under supernatural agency" (*Biog. Lit.*, Chap. XIV).

It seems possible, then, that the completion of "The Ancient Mariner" and the new partnership generated by the plan to go to Germany together revived the collaborative efforts of the fall of 1797, and the supernatural-superstition parallel between Wordsworth's "The Thorn" and "Goody Blake and Harry Gill" and Coleridge's "Ancient Mariner" encouraged more such investigation in the joint "The Three Graves," Wordsworth's *Peter Bell*, and

Coleridge's "Christabel." A curse motif[5] running through
these poems would give the group substantial unity, and
the two kinds of treatment of the openly supernatural
versus the pseudo-supernatural of superstition, resembles
the kind of division of labor Coleridge later talked about.
The idea is exciting, and would have justified Wordsworth's writing Cottle on May 9 that he had "lately been
busy with another plan" than the proposals concerning
"Salisbury Plain"—proposals which do not fit neatly into
this context. This truly balanced collaborative effort would
explain the stance Coleridge attributes to Wordsworth in
a letter to Cottle of May 28–June 4:

> Wordsworth & I have *maturely weigh'd* our proposal, & this
> is our answer—W. would not object to the publishing of Peter
> Bell *or* the Salisbury Plain, singly; but to the publishing of *his*
> *poems* in two volumes he is decisevely repugnant & oppugnant—
> He deems that they would want variety &c &c—if this apply in
> his case, it applies with tenfold force to mine.—We deem that the
> volumes offered to you are to a certain degree *one work, in*
> *kind tho' not in degree,* as an Ode is one work—& that our
> different poems are as stanzas, good relatively rather than abso-
> lutely:—Mark you, I say *in kind* tho' not in degree.— (*Letters,*
> I, 411-2)

All these protestations of Wordsworth's repugnance at
separate publication are curious in the light of earlier plans
for just that, and of Dorothy's and William's subsequent
references to the volume as *his* poems. And this insistence
on the unity of *one work* is odd in relation to the spread
of the volume which resulted. Yet Wordsworth bought this
idea at the time, as appears from his statement in the
Preface:

> For the sake of variety and from a consciousness of my own
> weakness I was induced to request the assistance of a Friend. . . .
> I should not, however, have requested this assistance, had I not
> believed that the poems of my Friend would in a great measure
> have the same tendency as my own, and that, though there
> would be found a difference, there would be found no discordance

in the colours of our style; as our opinions on the subject of poetry do almost entirely coincide.[6]

That their opinions on poetry did not almost entirely coincide Coleridge made clear in his *Biographia Literaria* and Wordsworth perhaps recognized earlier, since he dropped the passage from the Preface after 1805. At the moment, however, there was a great sense of common theme and common purpose. Probably most of the curse poems were still expected to be in the collection at the time of Coleridge's letter, since he speaks of volumes in the plural, and Cottle says that he had recommended two volumes.

Between Wordsworth's letter to Cottle on May 9 and Coleridge's of about June 4, the publisher came to visit at Alfoxden, learned of the other plan Wordsworth had been busy about, and made some agreements which finally led to the *Lyrical Ballads*. In his *Early Recollections* he records:

I spent a week with Mr. C. and Mr. W. at Allfoxden house, and during this time, (besides the reading of MS. Poems) they took me to Limouth, and Linton, and the Valley of Stones. . . . At this interview it was determined, that the volume should be published under the title of "Lyrical Ballads," on the terms stipulated in a former letter: that this volume should not contain the poem of "Salisbury Plain," but only an extract from it; that it should not contain the poem of "Peter Bell," but consist rather of sundry shorter poems, and, for the most part, of pieces more recently written. I had recommended two volumes, but one was fixed on, and that to be published anonymously. It was to be begun immediately, and with the "Ancient Mariner"; which poem I brought with me to Bristol. (I, 314-15)

There is no telling how much of this Cottle deduced from later events and how much he remembered from that "interview," since Coleridge's letter makes it appear that the decision to have only one volume had not yet been made. But the publisher was correct about the collection's consisting chiefly of "pieces more recently written" and he evidently took at least "The Ancient Mariner" with him back to Bristol, along with some sort of agreement which he apparently had not yet entirely accepted, since Coleridge's letter directs: "However, I waive all *reasoning*; & simply state it as an unaltered opinion, that you should proceed as before, with the ancient Mariner" (*Letters*, I, 412).

The exact date of Cottle's visit is not clear, but it was probably May 22-30. One difficulty is that this time span overlaps with that of Hazlitt's famous meeting with the poets, and neither Cottle nor Hazlitt mentions the other in any of his accounts of their experiences. It appears, however, that by the end of May a die of some sort had been cast. Dorothy had, as we have seen, several times before this said that her brother was about to publish some poems, but there is a most definite tone in her letter of May 31 telling Richard their brother had "sold his poems very advantageously": "William has now some poems in the Bristol press, and he wishes to superintend the printing of them" (*EY*, p. 219). Therefore the Wordsworths were planning to take lodgings in Bristol for a short time. Although Dorothy admits that the wish to be with friends —probably the James Loshes, who had taken a house at Shirehampton, about five miles from Bristol, on the Severn —contributed to the desire to be in the area, Wordsworth's intention of superintending the press shows an interesting concern for the welfare of the volume. He injected a comment on printing in a letter of Coleridge to Cottle, at a point where Coleridge had been pleading for "18 lines to the page, the lines closely printed, certainly, *more closely* than those of the Joan [Southey's *Joan of Arc*, which Cottle had printed]": here Wordsworth inserted, "Oh by all means closer! W. Wordsworth" (*Letters*, I, 412).

Just how much superintending of the press he did is unknown, but Wordsworth was several times in the Bristol

area during the next two or three months. About June 10 he
went to Bristol, probably taking to Cottle the copy for
"Expostulation and Reply" and "The Tables Turned," and
visited at Shirehampton for several days. On July 2—after
they had given up Alfoxden on June 25 and gone by Nether
Stowey to store some of their possessions at Coleridge's,
William and Dorothy went on to Bristol and spent several
days with Cottle and the Loshes before setting out, probably on July 10, for the Wye Valley, on the expedition
which produced "Lines Composed a Few Miles Above
Tintern Abbey." Wordsworth probably finished this poem
on July 13 and maybe gave it to Cottle the same day—the
last piece of his "stock of poetry" to be included in the first
edition of the *Lyrical Ballads*. A few days later, on July 18,
Dorothy informed someone, possibly Mary: "William's
poems are now in the press; they will be out in six weeks."
(*EY*, p. 226).

The press, however, has its delays and frustrations, and
these must have been a fairly hectic six weeks: D.F. Foxon
has ingeniously worked out a history of the printing of the
Lyrical Ballads from a careful study of pin points, water
marks, and paper of eight copies of the first issue of the
first edition.[7] The title page read:

LYRICAL BALLADS,/WITH/*A FEW OTHER POEMS*./
BRISTOL:/PRINTED BY BIGGS AND COTTLE,/
FOR T.N. LONGMAN, PATERNOSTER-ROW,
LONDON./1798.

The predominant collation of the thirteen known surviving
copies of this issue indicates curious irregularities: $\pi 1 \, 2\pi^4$
$[A]^8$ B–C^8 D^8(–D8) χ^4 $[E]^8$(–E1, 2) F–N^8 O^4(–O4). The
page numbering reflects these peculiarities: [63], 64-9, two
pages unnumbered, 70-84. Obviously, something happened to cause D8–E2 to be cancelled and replaced by χ^4;
and since the cancel contained one leaf or two pages

more than the original, there are two additional pages, which are kept from throwing the pagination off by simply being left unnumbered.

Four copies preserving this early state have survived to show us what happened; we can only guess why. Apparently Cottle's printers set up and printed the body of the volume, A-N; then ran off O, consisting of the last page of the text (O1), an errata page (O2), a page of advertisements (O3), and possibly a title page (which has not survived) showing Cottle as the publisher. Probably later, on what looks like different paper, they set up and proofed a contents page and a title page showing the poems to be printed in Bristol by Biggs and Cottle for Longman, and issued advance copies in this form. This first state included "Lewti, Or the Circassian Love-Chaunt," a poem Coleridge elaborated from "Beauty and Moonlight, An Ode *Fragment*," which Wordsworth wrote, probably in 1786, to a "Mary" who was perhaps Mary Hutchinson. Coleridge changed Mary to Lewti, "Winander's stream" to "Tamaha's stream," added the refrain, and expanded the conventional love theme from 36 to 83 lines. This poem, therefore, represented something of the kind of collaboration that Coleridge had been wanting, and in that sense appeared especially appropriate to his concept of the volume as "one work." Yet it was dropped from the collection, and the purpose of the χ gathering was to substitute Coleridge's "The Nightingale, A Conversation Poem, April, 1798." Set up together with χ was 2π, containing the Advertisement and a new contents leaf on the recto of $2\pi4$.

Coleridge had already published "Lewti" in Daniel Stuart's *Morning Post*, on April 13, 1798, over the signature "*Nicias Erythraeus*," and the assumption usually made (apparently going back to an unsupported assertion by T.J. Wise)[8] is that the poets decided to withdraw it from the *Lyrical Ballads* because this publication compromised the

anonymity they desired for their collection. Coleridge
was particularly insistent with Cottle, who evidently argued that affixing the poets' names would help the sale of
the volume:

As to anonymous Publications, depend on it, you are deceived.—
Wordsworth's name is nothing—to a large number of persons
mine *stinks*—The Essay on Man, Darwin's Botanic Garden, the
Pleasures of memory, & many other most popular works were
published anonymously.—(*Letters*, I, 412)

Wordsworth, on the other hand, wrote Coleridge in
December 1799, "Take no pains to contradict the story that
the L.B. are entirely yours. Such a rumour is the best
thing that can befall them."[9] It is unlikely that the poets
expected to keep their authorship secret. Of course their
friends like Losh knew, and undoubtedly others as well.
Southey, whose review in the *Critical Review* we recall
Wordsworth did not consider friendly, wrote at least to
William Taylor of Norwich (September 5, 1798) and C.W.
Williams Wynn in London (December 17) telling them the
identity of the authors. Probably Wordsworth and Coleridge were chiefly interested in keeping their names off
the title page, particularly *two* names. The Advertisement
speaks of "the author," deliberately giving the impression
that one poet is responsible for the whole. At this time the
poets were intent upon preserving the unity of their
"experiment," and I think it is at least as likely that
"Lewti" was dropped because that poem did not fit into
the experiment as because it breached the volume's anonymity. Why should the poets have belatedly remembered
the prior publication of "Lewti" and been so much concerned that Daniel Stuart and his circle knew that Coleridge
was the author? As their project solidified, however, they
might well have become more convinced of the integrity
and originality of their purpose, and decided that "The

Nightingale" was more appropriate to that purpose. Perhaps it is significant that gathering 2π was apparently set up at the same time as χ, which indicates that the Advertisement was in some sense contemporaneous with the insertion of "The Nightingale." Of course the announcement of the experiment could have been intended all along,[10] and even have been written before the substitution, but the interesting fact remains that it was just then printed. May not the Advertisement have been an afterthought, a product of the impulse which threw out "Lewti" and replaced it with the much more original and superior "The Nightingale"?[11] The romantic, sentimental conventionality of "Lewti" is underscored by the comment the editor of the *Morning Post* saw fit to attach to it:

> . . . it may afford the mind a temporary relief to wander to the magic haunts of the Muses, to bowers and fountains which the despoiling powers of war have never visited, and where the lover pours forth his complaint, or receives the recompense of his constancy. . . . (*Poems*, ed. E.H. Coleridge, p. 253n.)

In language and content this is not the kind of thing with which the experiment was concerned.

Some indication of the confusion, vacillation, or license which existed at Cottle's print shop is the fact that one surviving copy of the first issue, a copy which belonged to Southey, contains both "Lewti" and "The Nightingale," and also both tables of contents. This copy, however, may have been an intentional bibliographical rarity, concocted by Cottle as a gift to Southey.[12] A still greater oddity is a copy which contains "The Nightingale" and also, inserted before χ in the position of "Lewti," a single leaf, the recto unnumbered and the verso numbered 63*, containing a poem called "Domiciliary Verses" by Dr. Thomas Beddoes, a notable Bristol physician and friend of Coleridge and Cottle. Foxon has suggested that Cottle thought of these verses as a substitute for "Lewti" after it had been decided to drop that poem, but before "The Nightingale" had been selected as a replacement, got Beddoes' permission to use his poem, and then after that plan fell through printed up a special presentation copy for the doctor as a consolation. Cottle was quire presumptuous enough to have taken so much upon himself. But if "Domciliary Verses" had been intended to take the place of "Lewti," we would expect the pages to be numbered 63-4, not [62*] 63*. The pagination suggests an indicated duplication of page numbers for superfluous insertion. Of course Cottle could, as Foxon suggests, have printed up the single leaf for insertion in Beddoes' copy only after the plan to substitute it had been abandoned and therefore after the pagination appropriate to substitution would have applied. He might just as well, however, have done the same thing because he thought Beddoes' poem echoed the domestic themes of "The Nightingale," and maybe even vainly tried to get the authors to incorporate the doctor's verses.

Dorothy's "six weeks" were just about up when William wrote to Cottle from London on August 28, worrying because their boxes had not come, asking if the publisher could help him sell some valuable copies of Gilpin's *Tours*, and requesting another letter of introduction to Longman, since they forgot to bring one previously furnished—and never specifically mentioning *Lyrical Ballads*. Perhaps we can infer that when the Wordsworths left Bristol about the middle of August *Lyrical Ballads* was printed, or nearly enough so that Wordsworth felt no need to ask about it on August 28. The problem now was the publisher, or at least the London agent. Possibly the letter of introduction to T.N. Longman, a London publisher who had a partnership with Owen Rees, a Bristol bookseller and neighbor of Cottle's, betokens an agreement to sound out Longman on taking over the *Lyrical Ballads*. Maybe Wordsworth even carried a copy neatly made up with Longman's name on the title page to show him what he would be getting.

All Cottle's dealings with Wordsworth and Coleridge had suggested that he would himself be the publisher of *Lyrical Ballads:* he asserted that intention in a letter as late as October 2, and in 1837 claimed that he indeed published the work, but what he called "the heavy [*i.e.* slow] sale," induced him "to part with the largest proportion of the impression of Five hundred, at a loss, to Mr. Arch, a London bookseller."[13] The title page of the Bristol issue, however—printed "for T.N. Longman" instead of the usual "sold by T.N. Longman" for a mere outlet—suggests that when Cottle had that page set up he either thought or hoped that Longman would publish the book, or at least, to use a term he later applied to Arch, become his "agent." He had sold Longman the second edition of Southey's *Joan of Arc* (1798). To put the most favorable interpretation on his action, he may have anticipated that he was himself going out of business in about a year and thought the connection with Longman would be useful to the poets. To take a more cynical view, as do Hutchinson[14] and Foxon, he may have received from Southey advance notice of the critical opinions later expressed in his *Critical Review* commentary, along with advice to unload an unsaleable article. More likely, he just needed the cash and wanted to repeat a pattern which had worked with *Joan of Arc.* In any event, Longman did not publish the 1798 *Lyrical Ballads.* Coleridge wrote Southey later that Longman had come to regret the *Joan of Arc* deal and was "indisposed to similar negociations" (December 24, 1799)—possibly Coleridge was remembering the *Lyrical Ballads* negotiations. Maybe Longman was dubious about being able to make any money on this "experiment"—since about a year later when Cottle went out of business and sold all his copyrights in a package to Longman, the latter counted the value of the *Lyrical Ballads* as nothing and gave it back to Cottle at his request, so that he could present it to Wordsworth.

Whether or not Cottle himself then published the book in Bristol is not clear. The answer more or less hinges on the definition of "publish." As we have seen, Cottle's later statement suggests that he did publish the work, and then turned the issue over to Arch because the sale was "heavy." Southey obviously thought the book was out by September 5, when he wrote William Taylor, "Have you seen a volume of *Lyrical Ballads*, etc?"[15] His remarks on the contents indicate that he himself had seen a copy, or at least advance sheets. On September 13, however, Dorothy is very definite in telling an unknown correspondent that her brother's poems were "printed, but not published." The next day the Wordsworths took ship from London and on September 15 sailed from Yarmouth to Hamburg. On October 3 William wrote to Henry Gardiner: "I do not yet know what is become of my poems, that is, who is their publisher. It was undecided when I came off."[16] It is possible that Southey, having seen only advance material, was mistaken in thinking the book published; or that the Wordsworths, out of touch with Cottle and what was happening in Bristol, were a little behind time on events.

Apparently, part of the cause of the confusion was some activity on Wordsworth's part in London to find a publisher for himself, or indeed to change his publisher by means of maneuvering which smacks of a certain disingenuousness. Joseph Johnson of Saint Paul's Church Yard had published Wordsworth's *An Evening Walk* and *Descriptive Sketches* back in 1793, and was evidently a most attractive person. Shortly before leaving for Germany, Coleridge introduced himself to Johnson and reported the bookseller received him "civilly the first time, cordially the second, affectionately the third—& finally took leave of me with tears in his eyes— He is a worthy Man."[17] Possibly Coleridge urged Wordsworth to give their volume of poems to this affectionate and worthy man. Possibly Wordsworth needed little urging to take up the former connection; he might have reasoned that a London publisher would be advantageous in promoting the sale of the *Lyrical Ballads*. Such a development would be all the more likely if Wordsworth had known about and participated in negotiations with Longman which fell through.

At any rate, Wordsworth discussed the matter with Johnson, and deliberately neglected to tell him that the poems had been sold to Cottle. Having come to some sort of tentative agreement with the London publisher, he wrote Cottle on September 14 or 15 a letter which has not survived, asking the Bristol publisher to turn the *Lyrical Ballads* over to Johnson, and draw upon Richard Wordsworth to be repaid any advances he had made. The poet was in fact trying to buy back the copyright. According to Wordsworth's memory, he frankly told Cottle that the London publication might be more profitable to the authors, for he wrote Cottle soon after his return to England in May 1799—when, curiously, Wordsworth still did not know what had happened to *Lyrical Ballads*—"The day before I left England I wrote to you to request that you would transfer your right to the *Lyrical Ballads* to Mr. Johnson, on account of its being likely to be very advantageous to me" (*EY*, p. 259). And evidently, Wordsworth assumed that Cottle would have no objection to such a transfer, possibly because of the overtures to Longman; although if this was the case, it is a little odd that the poet does not mention the fact in his letters to his brother or the publisher. It is possible that he considered the Longman negotiations, if he knew about them, to be in a different category. In any event, he thought Cottle would acquiesce to his request, as is demonstrated by the fact that about the same time that he sent it to Cottle he also addressed a note to Johnson, asking him to deliver to Richard Wordsworth "6 copies of Lyrical Ballands [sic] for my friends"; and Richard made a memorandum "to receive from Johnson Booksell." as if he expected monies from that source.[18]

Cottle, however, either really persuaded himself that Wordsworth's true motivation was to spare him loss, and he should not accept the gallant offer, or got his back up because Wordsworth entered into negotiations with another publisher regarding property which actually belonged to Cottle. He apparently did not bother trying to communicate with Wordsworth in Germany, but on October 2, 1798, wrote to Johnson:

I have received a letter from Mr. Wordsworth requesting me to give up my Interest in his Lyrical Ballads to you. By the tenor of his letter I perceive clearly he is influenced, in this request, by an apprehension that the sale may not be such as to answer my purpose in publishing. I however purchased them of him originally with the intention of being their publisher, and I still have the same wish, and accordingly have sent them to my Agent for that purpose. (*EY*, p. 675)

Richard Wordsworth was incensed by the tone of Cottle's letter, and included a copy in his report of Wordsworth's finances upon his return to England, saying the business required his "immediate attention." William replied that he saw nothing wrong with the letter except for "his use of the word purchase. As I expressly told him that I made no mention to Johnson of any *positive* agreement between him and me, out of delicacy *he* ought not to have mentioned this to Johnson" (*EY*, p. 260). In a letter to Cottle on June 2, Wordsworth says the same thing in accepting Cottle's explanation that he could not transfer the *Lyrical Ballads* to Johnson because he had already "entered into a treaty with Arch," but still regrets the loss of an opportunity to connect himself with Johnson and the likelihood of a better sale. The difference between Wordsworth's proposed deal with Johnson and Cottle's with Arch was that Wordsworth intended in fact to resell his poems, while Cottle merely sold most of an impression and kept the copyright. The second deal forestalled the first, although perhaps it need not have if Johnson was really interested.

Cottle notes a littly smugly: "A Reason for non-compliance, which satisfied Mr. W."[19]

If, as Wordsworth's letter and an attached memorandum of Cottle's written much later indicate, Cottle made his agreement to sell most of the first impression of *Lyrical Ballads* to Arch before he got Wordsworth's letter written on September 14 or 15, then he could hardly have had much opportunity to discover whether there was a "heavy sale." His whole statement should not, however, be discredited—as it is by Daniel[20] and Foxon—simply because he seems to attribute the transfer to bad reviews, none of which, of course, had then appeared. Since Cottle evidently considered himself the publisher of the volume by proxy after he had transferred the copies to Arch, despite the fact that the title page of the second issue carries the legend "Printed for J. & A. Arch, Gracechurch-Street," it is possible that he so considered himself at the time that Dorothy and William, then gone from Bristol, were thinking of the *Lyrical Ballads* as "printed but not published," and that Southey was in a sense correct in believing that the book was available by September 5. It may have been published in Cottle's mind since mid-August, so that he waited about a month before he got a London outlet.

Certainly some copies were getting around—Southey had one, as we have seen, and so did Hannah More; and the book was well enough known in literary circles in London that at the dinner table of Mrs. Barbauld—the blue-stocking poetess whose name struck Coleridge as a "pleonasm of nakedness"—there was a discussion of *Lyrical Ballads* at which John Pinkerton, unaware of Coleridge's connection with the anonymous volume, complained to him about the book. According to Grattan's report of the incident long afterwards, Coleridge said this happened "a few days after" *Lyrical Ballads* was "published," and it must, of course, have been before the poets and Dorothy set out for Yarmouth on their way to Germany, on September 14.[21] This suggests that although Wordsworth and Dorothy were still looking for a publisher, Coleridge like Cottle thought the book was published. Even if Coleridge's memory is off on the matter of technical publication, at least the book was "out." It is possible, however, as Foxon and Daniel suggest, that the work was never really published in Bristol—that only a few copies were circulated to friends. The wording of Cottle's letter to Johnson can bear the interpretation that the poems were still to be published by his agent. Losh's diary records on September 18 that he paid 8d carriage of a book "from Bristol," and the next day he read "Coleridge and Wordsworth's poems aloud" (*EY*, p. 227n.). Unless this is regarded as a pre-publication copy to a friend, the volume had been published at least by September 15 and probably, although not necessarily, in Bristol.

Still, Cottle's statement in the 1837 *Early Recollections* that the slow sale induced him to part with *Lyrical Ballads* at a loss to Arch is certainly at odds with the 1798 version of turning the issue over to his "agent," and probably neither is entirely accurate. Probably Cottle anticipated a slow sale, perhaps because of Southey's criticism, perhaps of his own assessment of the "experiment" and his other publishing experience; and being short of capital, he determined to recoup something of what he had invested in *Lyrical Ballads,* at the same time keeping the copyright and the potential at least of being the publisher and patron. It is perhaps significant that although he promised Wordsworth 30 guineas for the volume, he had paid only £9/11 by September 14.[22] Cottle was not a successful businessman, and he lost heavily on many of his publishing ventures.

At any rate, Cottle had a new title page printed and the issue bound in boards in Bristol before shipping it off to

Arch. On October 4 advertisements appeared in *The Times*, the *Morning Chronicle*, and the *Morning Herald* announcing:

This day is published, in small 8vo. price 5s, in boards,
LYRICAL BALLADS: With a few other poems.
Printed for John and Arthur Arch, No. 23, Gracechurch-street,
London.[23]

And in the October number of the *Critical Review*, probably published about the first of November, Southey's review of the *Lyrical Ballads* appeared. The little volume was finally launched, and the Wordsworths and Coleridge in Germany waited to hear of the fate of the great "experiment."

CHAPTER THREE

Critical Environment

of the *Lyrical Ballads*

The *Lyrical Ballads* came forth in a critical climate that was neatly balanced or markedly schizophrenic, depending on one's point of view. Critics writing in the *Monthly Review* in mid-1797, and in the *Monthly Magazine* in January of the same year, expressed opposing judgements. The *Review* writer complacently believed that "the experience of a few past years has abundantly proved to us, that never was there a time in which *English poetry* was cultivated with more genius, nor with happier effect, and if we still want *great works* to put in parallel with those of former eras, yet our *minor poets* (*minor* in bulk, not in merit) may be advantageously compared with those of any age" (XXIII, 278). The *Monthly Magazine* critic, on the other hand, sighed, "The region of Parnassus appears to have experienced the chilling influence of a severe season: its plants have of late been, for the most part, remarkably feeble and sickly."

The crux of the disagreement, however, perhaps lay in the critical ambivalence which provided a conflicting set of criteria for value judgements at the end of the eighteenth century. A *Monthly Review* commentator on Rev. Thomas Cole's *The Life of Hubert* (1797) wrote:

but other things are necessary to form a poet; such as an intuitive perception of everything striking and beautiful in nature,—the power of selecting those circumstances which delight the imagination or affect the heart, and felicity of language, in respect to propriety, elegance and harmony. Nothing can be more contrary to our ideas of poetry, than a familiarity of style bordering on coarseness, if not vulgarity. (XXIV, 102-3)

There we see the critical problem: a recognition of the power of emotion, of appeals to feeling ("intuitive perception," "striking," "delight the imagination or affect the heart"), and yet a potentially contrary requirement for "propriety, elegance and harmony."

To Wordsworth, of course, the heart spoke a familiar language which had its own proprieties, and an intuition of immediacy which could flirt with "coarseness, if not vulgarity." The central novelty of his little book was the relative consistency of his critical principle. In the 1798 "Advertisement" he called the *Lyrical Ballads* an "experiment" written "chiefly with a view to ascertain how far the language of conversation in the middle and lower classes of society is adapted to the purposes of poetic pleasure." He might have added the "thoughts and attitudes" and, as he did later in the Preface, the "incidents and situations" from "humble and rustic life." He did not indulge in the kind of double-think characteristic of the eighteenth century, in which "simplicity" was hailed as a goddess, but fashionably draped and exhibited on an elegant pedestal. His simplicity—which we will explore in some detail later—included rusticity extending to idiot boys. As he explained in a revealing letter to John Wilson, "I must content myself simply with observing that it is probable that the principle [sic] cause of your dislike to this particular poem lies in the *word* Idiot. If there had been any such word in our language, *to which we had attached passion*, as lack-wit, half-wit, witless &c I should certainly have employed it in preference but there is no such word."[1]

It is hard to understand exactly what Wordsworth means by words "to which we have attached passion," but the remark clearly puts him on the side of intense feeling, even at the cost of disturbing lowness. He also told Wilson that "the best measure" of human nature was to be found "by stripping our own hearts naked, and by looking out of ourselves to[wards me]n who lead the simplest lives most according to nature, men who [ha]ve never known false refinements." Of course, to be honest, "false refinements" rather begs the question—nobody would admit to favoring *false* refinements. But most critics of the time seemed to demand, stridently or moderately, some element of refinement: restraint, polish, control.

The "correctness" that Pope said so very late became the care of English poetry was still much the concern of critics when the *Lyrical Ballads* appeared. In a revealing critical satire, "The Art of Poetry, According to the Latest Improvements, by Sir Simon Swan," published the same year as Wordsworth and Coleridge's little volume, Joseph Fawcett lamented:

> Most critics, a phlegmatic, icy race,
> To cold correctness give perfection's place. . . .
> Passion be sure avoid: no gentle ear
> The shock of aught so boisterous knows to bear.

In his preface Fawcett retreated somewhat and complained that he had been misunderstood as satirizing correctness— he meant to attack "not correctness in the abstract, but correct dullness." Nevertheless, even if the correct critics were leery of boisterous "passion," even they seemed to desire *something* of spirit and feeling. There was a stirring under the crust of control.

This polarity in the standards of the day is interestingly revealed in the writing of contemporary magazine critics. One set of terms of approval most often met with in the journals of the day includes such words as "animated,"

"spirited," or the stronger "fire," "vigor" and "wild," or
softer "pathos" and "tenderness"—all of which are the
products of "fancy" and "sublimity," are marked by "bril-
liancy" and "glowing imagery," and are welcomed for
"novelty" and "originality." Another more or less opposite
contemporary set of words of praise, sometimes found in
the same journals and even used by the same critics,
includes "correct," "rational," "judgment," and "taste,"
which are supposed to produce the "chaste," "elegant,"
"charming," "easy," "graceful," or "suave," and result in
the "natural," "harmonious," and even "simple"—although, as we will see, the notions of simplicity were
complicated, and it could in a primitivistic sense be associated with the other pole.

Terms of abuse are similarly divided, sometimes, but not
always, reflecting the obverse of the counters of praise. On
one side are "affected," "extravagant," "pompous," "sentimental," "unintelligible" and even "incomprehensibly sublime," with a condemnation of "glitter," "inflation," and
"indelicacy." On the other hand are "cold," "feeble,"
"flat," "languid," "trite," with contempt for "familiarity."
It may be fruitful to see how these critical principles
worked to establish an environment for the *Lyrical Ballads.*
We will observe that polarity is common but fuzzy; the
terms shift, but various oppositions usually continue,
although some critics appear to admit a compromise
Golden Mean.

One of the most trenchant voices at the end of the
eighteenth century was that of the *Anti-Jacobin Review
and Magazine; or, Monthly Political and Literary Censor.*
Its critics were given to such bluntness as the remark that
Michael Wodhull "prostituted" his talents (March 1799) in
The Equality of Mankind: A Poem (1798); and as for
Romaine Joseph Thorn's *Lodon and Miranda* (1799), they
had "not perused a book so very absurd, in every point of
view" (April 1800). But they liked the balance of *The Irish*

Boy: A Ballad (1799): "simple, harmonious and pathetic, it gratifies the taste and strongly affects the feelings" (March 1799). And interestingly, they found that balance in *Lyrical Ballads:* "It has genius, taste, elegance, wit and imagery of the most beautiful kind" (April 1800). They liked "The Ancyent Marinere," "The Foster Mother's Tale," "Simon Lee," "The Idiot Boy" and "Goody Blake and Harry Gill," and concluded "indeed the whole volume convinces us that the author possesses a mind at once classic and accomplished."[2]

In July 1797 the *Analytical Review* could praise *English Lyrics* both for being "correct, elegant, and tender" and for displaying a "lively fancy"; and a month later it could applaud the "delicacy" of Charlotte Smith's *Elegiac Sonnets, and other Poems.* But the journal was willing to go only so far in the direction of delicacy, for T.S. Surr's *Christ's Hospital, a Poem* was in October condemned as "somewhat languid, and somewhat cold," while the Rev. John Sharpe's *The Church, A Poem* was given qualified approval because "executed with considerable spirit." In February 1798, John Gorton's *Britannia* was derisively put down with the caustic comment that if the author's loyalty "were not more fervid than his poetry, his Majesty would not have a worse subject in his dominions." And in March, J. Hucks' *Poems* were criticized as "destitute of that spirit, that glowing imagery, and variety of cadence, which is necessary to lead along the attention, and to charm the ear." The *Analytical* also attacked the "affected phraseology" of Thomas White's *Saint Guerdur's Well, a Poem;* it condemned "that sort of sublimity, the essence of which is to be incomprehensible" in *The Villain's Deathbed; or, The Times: a Poem* (July 1798); and it found the "whining monotonous melancholy" of Charles Lloyd and Charles Lamb's *Blank Verse* "extremely tiresome" (May 1798). It approved the favored poets of the day, acclaiming Samuel Rogers' *An Epistle to a Friend* for "harmony of verse . . .

delicacy of sentiment . . . simplicity of taste" (April 1798),
and praising the "great delicacy, taste and feeling" (Dec.
1798) of W.L Bowles' *Coombe Ellen; a Poem*. The editors
more or less summed up their critical position in a review
of three editions of William Cowper in September 1798,
with a definition of a poet which in some ways anticipates
Wordsworth's "What is a Poet?" insertion in the 1802
version of his Preface to the *Lyrical Ballads:*

With a vigorous and exercised imagination, he must possess a
peculiar quickness of apprehension, power of combination, ex-
quisiteness of sensibility, and rectitude of taste. Science must
enlarge his mental prospect, and language, in its changeful and
most beautiful forms, must sit upon his tongue. He must see with
eyes, which, commanding a wide horizon, present him with every
object distinctly defined, yet variously and splendidly coloured.

When the *Analytical* came to review the *Lyrical Ballads*
in December 1798, it could, therefore, with fair consistency, be on the whole pleased by the combination of
simplicity and sensibility. Of the "Advertisement" and its
announcement of the "experiment" the reviewer said,
"there is something sensible in these remarks, and they
certainly serve as a very pertinent introduction to the
studied simplicity, which pervades many of these poems."
He approved the non-melancholy treatment of the nightingale and, balancing his criteria, listed as among the poems
which "particularly pleased us from their character either
of simplicity or tenderness or both": "The Nightingale,"
"The Thorn," "The Mad Mother," "The Idiot Boy," and
"Goody Blake and Harry Gill"—the last of which he
printed. He was not, however, pleased with the "Ancient
Mariner"—seeing in it "more of the extravagance of a mad
german poet, than the simplicity of our ancient ballad
writers."

Wordsworth fared even better with the *British Critic*,
because that journal was less concerned about correctness
but was rather, like the poet, reacting against Erasmus

Darwin's brand of elegance. Its critics, although conservative politically, were less so aesthetically, and tended to be generous to new writers. Their chief tags were "animated" and "spirited." Not that these terms exhausted their critical vocabulary, or that their generosity extended to universal commendation: Joseph Fawcett's *Poems* are praised for "some very elegant and harmonious composition" (Nov. 1798), whereas the author of *The Warning, a poetical Address to Britons* is told that although his intentions are highly laudable, he "seems not to have any talent for poetry" (Dec. 1798). The *Epistle in Rhyme, to M.G. Lewis* (1798), however, is approved because of its "melody and polish" of lines "united with energy and spirit" (Aug. 1798). Joseph Budworth's *Windermere, a Poem* has "some spirited lines" on "the bold and striking scenes of Nature" (Aug. 1798), Joseph Cottle's *Malvern Hills, a Poem* shows "some marks of true poetic spirit" (Sept. 1798), and *Matriculation, A Poem* is "spirited enough" (Oct. 1798). Similarly, W.L. Bowles' *Coombe Ellen. A Poem* is "highly animated throughout" (Nov. 1798) and his *Song of the Battle of the Nile* is "highly animated and impressive" (Feb. 1799); *Naucratia, or, Naval Dominion. A Poem,* by the Laureate, Henry James Pye, is "truly spirited" and *Ode to Lord Nelson, on his Conquest of Egypt,* by Harmodius, is a "very spirited effusion" (Dec. 1798); Maurice's *Grove Hill, a descriptive Poem* is "very animated," and William Thomas Fitzgerald's *Nelson's Triumph; or, the Battle of the Nile: a Poem* is an "animated effusion" (June 1799).

With that beadroll of spirit and animation, the criteria at least came as no surprise when in the summary of poetry in the Preface to Vol. XIV (July-December 1799) the editors remark, "The work entitled *Lyrical Ballads* contains many specimens of original and animated poetry, nor does the author so often descend to the flat ground of mere conversation in rhyme as he seems to threaten in his Preface."

The review of the work in October, which has been ascribed to Wordsworth's friend Francis Wrangham,[3] is even more enthusiastic:

The attempt made in this little volume is one that meets our cordial approbation; and is an attempt by no means unsuccessful. The endeavor of the author is to recall our poetry, from the fanatical excess of refinement, to simplicity and nature. (XIV, 365)

The reviewer prefers "even the most unadorned tale" to "all the meretricious frippery of the *Darwinian* taste," and in this collection does not often find anything "too familiar, or deficient in dignity." Indeed, he believes all the poems "have merit, and many among them a very high rank of merit." It is noteworthy that the critic picks out for special approval some of the most "experimental" verses: "The Female Vagrant," "We Are Seven," "The Thorn," "The Idiot Boy," and "A Forsaken Indian Woman," the last of which he quotes in full.

The second edition of *Lyrical Ballads* brought from the *British Critic* an equally favorable review (February 1801; XVII, 125-31), probably by John Stoddart: "he has adopted a purity of expression, which, to the fastidious ear, may sometimes perhaps sound poor and low, but which is infinitely more correspondent with true feeling than what, by the courtesy of the day, is usually called poetical language" (p. 125). The critic does not deny that sometimes Wordsworth "goes so far in his pursuit of simplicity as to become flat or weak" (p. 131), but thinks the worth of the subjects "grows upon the reader" and the language is "prompted by the natural flow of passion" (p. 127). This reviewer, obviously, is more attuned to Wordsworth than were the critics of the *Anti-Jacobin* and *Analytical*, but he still approves *Lyrical Ballads* partly by seeing it in terms of the contemporary balance: "purity" and "passion."

The reception of *Lyrical Ballads* received in the *Monthly Mirror Reflecting Men and Manners, With strictures on their Epitome, the Stage,* is more surprising, for that journal's critical policy revolved or wavered uncertainly around the popular critical poles. William Gifford's *Baviad* and *Maeviad,* for example, are praised as "animated and correct," while Percival Stockdale's *The Invincible Island* is condemned as "flat and prosaic" (March 1798). Pye's *Naucratia* is hailed as "spirited and highly poetical," but Joseph Budworth's *Windermere* is dismissed as neither elegant nor "very striking" (June 1798)—although the broad-mindedness of the journal is indicated by its willingness to publish later another and more favorable review of Budworth's poems, sent in by a "much esteemed Correspondent" (July 1798). The precise content of the *Monthly Mirror's* critical terms is rendered further suspect by assertions that Charlotte Smith is "always simple, always elegant, always a poet" (Jan. 1798); that even the lightweight *Bubble and Squeak, a Galli-Mawfry of British Beef, with Chopp'd Cabbage of Gallic Philosophy and Radical Reform* and its successor *Crambe Repetita,* by George Huddesford, possess "a considerable share of poetical eminence" (Sept. 1799); and that Campbell's amazingly popular *The Pleasures of Hope* sparkles with "brilliant fancy" and "fervid imagination" (July 1799).

This curious mixture suggests little editorial consistency and perhaps does not justify any prediction. Still, in the light of the implied concept of what constitutes a "fervid imagination," such criteria as were later epitomized by the wholehearted approval of Anna Seward's *Original Sonnets* as examples of "the elegantly descriptive, the beautifully picturesque, and the sublimely moral" (May 1799), and the journal's usual emphasis on correctness—"elevation of thought and dignity of expression," as they put it later (review of Thomas Maurice's *Poems, Epistolary, Lyric, and Elegiacal,* November 1800)—one might reasonably have expected the *Monthly Mirror* to have been highly critical of Wordsworth and Coleridge's little volume. If their review was more favorable than one might expect,

given their fondness for elegance, it is probably because the
editor tended to value the simply elegant, and therefore
to nourish a particular dislike of some contemporary
poets' penchant for "a variety of far-sought, inappropriate,
and absurd epithets" (rev. of John Westbrooke Chandler's
Sir Hubert, September 1800). On this tack the *Mirror* could
applaud the *Lyrical Ballads:*

The author has certainly accomplished his purpose, and instead of
the pompous and high-sounding phraseology of the *Della Cruscan*
school, has produced sentiments of feeling and sensibility, expressed without affectation, and in the language of nature. If
this style were more generally adopted, it would tend to correct
that depraved taste, occasioned by an incessant *importation* from
the press of *sonnets* and other poems, which has already made
considerable inroads upon the judgment. (October 1798, p. 224)

It is significant that the specimen of the author's talents
which the reviewer offers is the relatively conventional
"Lines Left upon a Seat in a Yew-Tree."

An amusing footnote to the *Mirror's* criticism of "high-
sounding phraseology" comes in their review of Charles
Lloyd and Charles Lamb's *Blank Verse,* which is solemnly
pronounced "sufficiently altisonant, without being bom-
bastical" (August 1798). So much for the "language of
nature." And it is worth observing that in 1800 Bloomfield's *The Farmer's Boy* gets a most favorable review,
which ran over two months and praised his piety, humility,
morality, truth and "engaging simplicity"—without any
reference to Wordsworth in the context; Bloomfield is
compared instead to James Thomson (March-April 1800).
The *Mirror* did, however, praise the 1800 edition of *Lyrical
Ballads* for "energy of thought, pathos of sentiment, and
exquisite discrimination in selecting whatever is picturesque in imagery, or interesting in nature" (XI, 389-92),
although obscurity is recognized as arising from "a romantic search after simplicity." The reviewer liked the
"sweetly-simple" poem "We Are Seven," and even more

"The Old Cumberland Beggar," which displayed "all the moral pith and nervous force of Cowper."

The same familiar critical dichotomy appeared also in the *Critical Review or Annals of Literature*, which by 1798 was into its twenty-second volume. Robert Farren Cheetham's *Odes and Miscellanies*, the critic asserts, "displays little novelty in his ideas, and little judgment in the arrangement" (January 1798): novelty—judgment. By these standards the Rev. John Chetwood Eustace's *An Elegy to the Memory of the Rt. Hon. Edmund Burke* is praised as "harmonious," and Joseph Atkinson's *Kilarney, a Poem* condemned as "languid and uninteresting" (April 1798). Similarly, Henry James Pye's *Naucratia; or Naval Dominion* is criticized for lacking "life and vigor" and Samuel Rogers' *An Epistle to a Friend* approved for being "polished and elegant" (July 1798). The magazine's reviewers liked neither the "namby-pamby" style of Ambrose Philips nor the "tinsel glitter" of the Della Cruscan school, and disliked such epithets as *"dew-eyed* and *day-eyed,* the *pale-eyed* and *flame-eyed"* (review of Thomas Townshend's *Poems* [February 1798]). They welcomed A.S. Cottle's English verse translation of *Icelandic Poetry, or the Edda of Saemund,* however, because it provided the poet with "a variety of images pecularly adapted for poetry by their novelty, their strangeness, and their sublimity" (January 1798). If Charlotte and Sophia King (*Trifles of Helicon*) err by allowing the "splendour of epithet" to lure them from "the path of simplicity," even Richard Polwhele's *The Old English Gentleman* is guilty of some expressions which "perhaps border on indelicacy" (March 1798). It is the old story of decorous simplicity and elegant novelty.

To review the *Lyrical Ballads,* the *Critical* chose Robert Southey, whose own works had ranged from *Joan of Arc* to the first "Botany Bay Eclogues," so that he had a foot in the "simple" camp. He took the tack that the idea of the

experiment was all right, but the execution was unsatis-
factory: "The experiment', we think, has failed, not
because the language of conversation is little adapted to
'the purposes of poetic pleasure,' but because it has been
tried upon uninteresting subjects. Yet every piece discovers
genius; and, ill as the author has frequently employed his
talents, they certainly rank him with the best of living
poets" (October 1798). This reaction was unacceptable to
Wordsworth, who thought that since Southey knew that
the purpose of his brother-in-law Coleridge's collaboration
was to make money, if he could not assist in that purpose,
he should at least keep quiet. But Southey, for all his
youthful revolutionism, was essentially an orderly and
decorous man, both a product and a supporter of the
balanced aesthetic. He considered the "Idiot Boy" the most
experimental poem, and declared that it resembled "a
Flemish picture in the worthlessness of its design and the
excellence of its execution." With "The Thorn" he was
"altogether displeased," and he thought "Goody Blake and
Harry Gill" possibly promoted popular belief in witchcraft!
What he liked best was "Tintern Abbey"—"on reading this
production, it is impossible not to lament that he should
have condescended to write such pieces as the Last of the
Flock, the Convict, and most of the ballads." However we
may be inclined to sympathize with this point of view, the
significant thing to note here is that the relatively liberal
Critical Review and the potential "laker" Southey were
actually less disposed to accept the "experiment" than were
the *Analytical Review* and the *British Critic*. It is the poem
least simple in style and diction which Southey, and other
critics, found most admirable.

The familiar critical balancing act with similar results is
performed by the *Monthly Review*. "But surely the term
'whetstone' conveys an idea too much beneath the dignity
of poetry," one of their critics declared in a comment on
Robert Farren Cheetham's *Odes and Miscellanies* (XXVI,

94). At the same time, neither could the journal approve of A. Peterkin's opening line in *Britannia's Tears, A Vision:* "Tenebrious gloom obscures the dismal night." This, they pointed out, amounted to "Dark darkness darkened the dark" (XXXI, 320). On the one hand they objected to artificial elevation of poetry, suggesting that a general property of contemporary blank verse seemed to be "obscurity" (XXII, 85). On the other hand, they were opposed to any undignified lowering of poetry, complaining that in *Poems* (1799) Southey "attempted to make the Muse descend a step lower, and has, in reality, brought her to the level of prose" (XXXI, 262). As they put it in another context, "common thoughts expressed in common words will not constitute the *language of the gods*, as the antients called poetry" (XXVIII, 106).

One summary of the *Monthly's* poetic criteria appears in a review of W.L. Bowles' little book, *Hope: An Allegorical Sketch, on Recovering slowly from Sickness:* "He possesses many of the requisites of a true poet; pathos, distinct imagery, elegant diction, and melody in his versification" (XXIII, 105). But beside that defense of elegance, put the statement that Joseph Fawcett's *Poems* show in "vigour of imagination, splendour of imagery, and force of expression" that he had few superiors among his contemporaries (XXVIII, 269), and it becomes more apparent that the *Monthly* sits on the golden mean fence of the day. Pye's *Carmen Seculare* is "truly poetical" because it displays "both judgment and taste, it abounds with a grand and suitable imagery; and the verse flows with graceful dignity" (XXXI, 304). As the century turned, *Monthly* critics became increasingly insistent in their double-edged vigilance, fuming early in 1800: "the fashionable affectation of simple diction is more disquieting than the over-refinement of the last age" (XXXI, 321). In their review of the *Annual Anthology* for 1799, they saw the villain as affectation itself: "We have attacked nothing but affectation, the moral poison of every species of composition. In whatever form this enemy of good poetry may appear, whether in overstrained refinement or in vulgar simplicity, we shall use our utmost endeavours to expose it" (XXXI, 363).

The *Monthly's* review of *Lyrical Ballads* in June 1799 fits into this context, with the additional factor that the reviewer has been identified as Dr. Charles Burney,[4] father of Madame D'Arblay (Fanny Burney), who had been lady-in-waiting to the Queen, and whose husband was a French emigré. Therefore Dr. Burney was understandably perturbed about the social implications in "The Female Vagrant" and even "The Old Man Travelling," and the criticisms of the established order conceivably discernible in "Goody Blake and Henry Gill," "The Last of the Flock," and "The Convict." Even "Tintern Abbey," although "poetical, beautiful and philosophical" is "somewhat tinctured with gloomy, narrow and unsociable ideas." But to the main subject of the experiment, Burney takes the expected line against affected simplicity: "Though we have been extremely entertained with the fancy, the facility, and (in general) the sentiments, of these pieces, we cannot regard them as *poetry*, of a class to be cultivated at the expense of a higher species of versificaiton, unknown in our language at the time when our elder writers, whom this author condescends to imitate, wrote their ballads" (XXIX, 202). Burney thinks that Percy's *Reliques* are interesting enough because they were ancient and surprising, but to imitate them is like going back to eating acorns!

Interestingly, there is no immediate evidence that the *Monthly* critics saw Wordsworth as the leader of the affectedly simple school. When Southey is taken to task for his triviality of thought and expression, he is said to have been "seduced by the brilliant and dangerous eccentricities of Cowper" (XXXI, 262). And when Robert Bloomfield's verses in *The Farmer's Boy* are praised for his having "contrived to embellish their rusticity and madness with a harmony of numbers" and "to soften the harshness of minute detail by blending apt and picturesque descriptions"

(XXXIII, 52), no reference is made to *Lyrical Ballads* by way of contrast. In 1802 the *Monthly* greeted "Vol. II" with a three-sentence review which expressed a hope of seeing more of "this natural, easy sentimental Bard, in his pensive rambles through the wilds and groves of his truly poetic, though somewhat peculiar imagination" (XXXVIII, 209).

When the other *Monthly*—the *Monthly Magazine and British Register*—on the same page criticizes Robert Merry's *Pains of Memory* for not being "entirely free from the glitter of affected language" and praises Boyd's *Poems* for "considerable command of elevated diction" (January 1797), it appears to be on the familiar not-so-simple-simplicity standard.

But the *Monthly Magazine* from its beginning in 1796 seemed to have a disposition that would be favorable to Wordsworth's experiment. In March of that first year it published an account of Bürger's work which remarked on his "rejection of the conventional phraseology of regular poetry, in favour of popular forms of expression, caught by the listening artist from the voice of agitated nature"— phrasing which sounds almost as if it might have come out of Wordsworth's Preface to *Lyrical Ballads*. Moreover, in March and April the journal printed William Taylor's translations of Bürger's "Lenora" and "The Lass of Fair Wone," which may have influenced "The Idiot Boy" and the "curse poems" respectively;[5] and later in the year it found genius in Coleridge's *Poems* and gave a wreath of honor to Southey's *Joan of Arc*. In the Supplement to their January-June 1797 collected volume, the editors print an essay "On the Characteristics of Poetry" which had been read to a Liverpool Literary Society in 1794, but again sounds rather like the Preface:

A poet must be a man of delicate perceptions and strong feelings; and he may be said to have attained the summit of his art, when he is master of vivid phraseology, that will operate as a conductor, and communicate to his reader, in the highest possible degree, those feelings by which he is himself animated. (III, 543)

Some affinity with the *Monthly Magazine* is also suggested by the fact that, as we have seen, Wordsworth told Isabel Fenwick that he and Coleridge began work on "The Ancient Mariner" with the intention of publishing it in that journal. Politically liberal to radical, it was published by Richard Phillips, edited until 1806 by Dr. John Aikin, and included William Godwin, Dr. Wolcot, and William Taylor among its contributors.

After all this, it is somewhat disappointing that the "Retrospect of Domestic Literature" at the end of 1798 should give much attention to William Lisle Bowles, and dismiss *Lyrical Ballads* briefly and inaccurately, if not unkindly: "The author of '*Lyrical Ballads*', has attempted to imitate the style of our old English versifiers, with unusual success; '*The Auncient Mariners*' [*sic*], however, on which he particularly prides himself, is in our opinion, a particular exception; some of his pieces are beautiful, but others are stiff and laboured." (VI, 514). The *Monthly Magazine's* critiques for the next few years find no occasion to refer further to *Lyrical Ballads*, and reveal that their favorites are Bowles; Seward—"at once so vivid, glowing, and correct" (June 1799); Campbell—of "uniformly correct and majestic style" (Dec. 1799); and Bloomfield. Even Erasmus Darwin is treated with respect, despite his fault of "dazzling and excessive polish" (July 1803).

The Philological Society of London published the *European Magazine and London Review*, allegedly "Containing the Literature, History, Politics, Arts, Manners and Amusements of the Age." In such a welter there was relatively little room for poetry—a monthly "Poetry" section and a few reviews. The reviews exhibit the characteristic tasteful-animation complex we have seen. As a commentator on Thomas Maurice's *Poems Epistolary, Lyric, and Elegiacal* neatly sums it up: "correct, spirited and unborrowed" (June 1800). Anna Seward's much-hailed

Original Sonnets on various Subjects was similarly praised for "vigour and elegance" (XXXV, 323), and the loyal critic of Henry James Pye's *Carmen Seculare for the Year 1800* stood up for the Laureat:

The real wits and the would be pretenders are generally in full cry against the unfortunate Laureate, and candour is silenced and drowned in senseless clamour. The present performance we, however, pronounce to be truly poetical; it exhibits marks of judgment as well as taste, displays imagery, sublime and agreeable to the subject. The verse also is smooth and flowing. (April 1800)

From this set of standards, this journal's contribution to the critical reception of the *Lyrical Ballads* was to publish in the poetry section for September 1801 as an implied defense of judgment and taste, a poem of thirty-one quatrains called "Barnham Downs; or Goody Grizzle and her Ass. A Lyrical Ballad, in the Present Fashionable Stile." It was signed "Rusticus, Cottage of Mon Repose, near Canterbury, Kent, August 27, 1801." From the same address the *European* also published epistles from "John, the Hermit" about the virtues of solitude. This "lyrical ballad" tells the sad tale of Goody's adventures as she comes home from the market one day:

> It came to pass, it came to pass,
>   Oh tale of wondrous dole!
> That Goody Grizzle and her Ass
>   Fell plump into a hole.
>
> All in a hole, all in a hole,
>   Down, down they tumbled plump,
> And Grizzle's nose, alas, poor soul!
>   Lay close to Dapple's rump.

The good dame heard a crack and thought it was a ghost:

> But ah! it was nor ghost, nor groan!
>   It was a rumbling roar;
> A kind of broken-winded tone
>   She ne'er had heard before.

It was—it was—oh, sad mishap!
    The Ass in 'doleful dumps,'
With whoop whoop whoop, and clap clap clap
    Was thund'ring out his trumps!

Nor wind alone, oh lack-a-day,
    Burst forth at each explosion!
Six quarts of half-digested hay
    Composed the od'rous lotion!

Of course Wordsworth never approached the scatology of this parody—he probably would have been shocked at the thought—and "Rusticus" is getting part of his fun from ridiculing the repetitive simple language. His main target, however, is clearly the subject matter: the low, inappropriate, mean and distasteful subject matter.

Flowers of Literature; for 1801 & 1802: or Characteristic sketches of Human Nature and Modern Manners, To which is added, a General View of Literature during that Period, With Notes, Historical, Critical and Explanatory, By the Rev. F. Prevost, and F. Blagdon, Esq., is not so formidable a work as its title promises. It seems to have taken no explicit notice of Wordsworth, although the third edition of Lyrical Ballads came out in 1802 and poems from it were reprinted in other journals during this period. Indeed, Flowers is a collection of short excerpts, mostly in prose; and the verse is generally anonymous and sentimental. The editors provide an "Alphabetical List of the Principal Publications, from which the Present Volume has been Composed: to which are added a few Brief Criticisms on their Respective Merits." How the editors viewed the poetic production of 1801-1802 is indicated by the six volumes of verse they listed:

Bread; or the Poor: a poem. By Mr. Pratt — "rich, varied, and affecting colours."
Idyls: in two parts. By Edward Atkyns Bray — "caught the true character of this kind of poetry."

Miscellaneous Poems. By W.F. Fitzgerald — "towering flights of
   poetry . . . sensibility and pathetic powers."
*Nautical Odes, or, Poetical Sketches, designed to commemorate
   the achievements of the British Navy* — "effusions."
Poetical Epistle to Sir George Beaumont, Bart. By Wm. Sotheby
   — "ranks among the first British bards."
Peasant's Fate; a Rural Poem: with Miscellaneous Poems. By Wm.
   Halloway — "harmonious versification."

In the next two years *Flowers* found more poetry worthy of
its list—that for 1804 included sixty-one titles under
"poetry"—but the critical standards appear to have remained about the same. There is the typical appreciation
of "pathos" and "polish" (review of Luke Booker's *Calista;
or, a Picture of Modern Life,* 1803).

   The *Imperial Review; or London and Dublin Literary
Journal,* which began publication in 1804, offers another
interesting example of the golden mean combination of
taste and genius, and also an indication of a solidifying
attack on Wordsworth as the exponent of excess. Percy
they consider overvalued, and Scott's *The Lay of the Last
Minstrel* they think reveals "the cold and groveling pursuits
of antiquarianism" (January 1805). Charles Grant's *A
Poem on the Restoration of Learning in the East,* however,
"is a generous effort to rescue poetry from her present
degradation, by furnishing a specimen of classical sublimity" (June 1805). And the enlarged 1805 edition of
Grahame's *The Sabbath* was hailed as a work of "chaste
and vigorous imagination" (February 1805). One of the
agents of this lamented degradation was held to be Erasmus
Darwin. Charles A. Elton's *Poems,* we are told, were
"formed on the vitiated models of the Darwin school . . . a
fashionable but a bad style of poetry" (November 1804).
Another agent clearly was Wordsworth, as appears from
the review of Thomas Brown's *Poems:*

Some of our latest poets, from what motive we cannot guess,
have laboured, with a sort of retrograde industry, in Tales of

Wonder, Lyrical Ballads, &c to barbarize our versification, and, by returning to the lame stanza and prosaic flow of obsolete compositions, to undo the toils of those who have reduced us to correctness. (November 1804)

Here the emphasis seems to be on correctness of versification, and Wordsworth is condemned more for his style than for his subject matter. It is interesting also that Wordsworth should be associated with Tales of Wonder (probably a reference to Monk Lewis' volume of that title published in 1801), since they represent the very "gross and violent stimulants" which he said in his 1800 Preface he was revolting against. Perhaps this critic was thinking chiefly of "The Rime of the Ancient Mariner," which Wordsworth continued to print, although acknowledging it as the work of a friend; there are, however, superstitious and supernatural elements in Wordsworth's ballads despite his disclaimer: notably in "Goody Blake and Harry Gill" and "The Thorn."

The *New Annual Register or General Repository of History, Politics, and Literature for the Year 1798* takes the standard middle-of-the-road position between vulgarity and refinement by quoting Nathan Drake's "Remarks on Pastoral Poetry, and Its Appropriate Diction, Imagery, and Incidents" from the popular *Literary Hours* published in 1798: "I am persuaded, however, that simplicity in diction and sentiment, a happy choice of rural imagery, such incidents and circumstances as may even now occur in the country, with interlocutors equally removed from vulgarity or considerable refinement, are all that are essential to success" (p. 101). The editors include in their "Poetry" section "Goody Blake and Harry Gill," and in their generally agreeable and commendatory section of reviews of modern English poetry, they sum up the *Lyrical Ballads* as the work of an author of "considerable talents":

Many of the ballads are distinguished by great simplicity and tenderness, and contain a very 'natural delineation of human passions, human characters, and human incidents.' With others we have been less satisfied, considering them to be unfortunate experiments, on which genius and labour have been misemployed. Of the remaining pieces some are highly beautiful and pleasing, and present us with passages which entitle the author to a very respectable rank among modern poets. (pp. 309-10)

Thus Wordsworth is made to fit innocuously into a middle position by the *New Annual Register.*

Not so by the *Poetical Register and Repository of Fugitive Poetry*, which takes a similar position but appears to make no specific reference to the *Lyrical Ballads*. In its volume for 1801 it does include Wordsworth's name in its "Chronological List of Living Poetical Writers, according to the date of their earliest Poetical Publication," assigning him the date 1800, and thus ignoring *Evening Walk* and *Descriptive Sketches*, which were published in 1793 with Wordsworth's name on the title pages, and associating him first with the *Lyrical Ballads* in the second edition, the first to bear his name. The standards of the *Register*, however, generally reflect the reigning dualism. Perhaps the editors tend to tilt more against the tinselly than the low, objecting to "the inflation of language, a fondness for dazzling imagery, and a redundance of epithet" in Mrs. Robinson's work, and rejoicing that W. Case Jr.'s taste is "unvitiated by those meretricious ornaments which too commonly disfigure the poetry of the present day" (*The Minstrel Youth, a Lyric Romance*) (pp. 433, 444). They repeat the common vocabulary in hailing the Rev. Brian Broughton's *Six Picturesque Views of North Wales, with Poetical Reflections* as "spirited, interesting, and harmonious"; W.L. Bowles' *The Sorrows of Switzerland; a Poem* as "highly animated and beautiful"; and William Boscawen's *Poems* as "elegant, correct and perspicuous." Similarly, they condemn *The Sweets of Society, a Poem* for being "languid and incorrect" (pp. 441, 443, 438). In their 1805 volume they even praise James Montgomery's *The Wanderer of Switzerland* for this interesting combination: "masculine yet elegant simplicity" (p. 485).

The *Gentleman's Magazine* devoted little time to verse and held a dour view of the contemporary poetic scene, indeed of much of the scene in general. It sounds quite current in its comment on *Matriculation, A Poem:* "Would to God a more *rigid discipline* was exercised within the walls of our Universities!" (October 1798). *Conversation, a Didactic Poem,* by William Cooke, elicited in the same month, "In this age of frivolous poetry, it affords us pleasure to meet with a work of taste and judgment." On a new publication of Glover's *Leonidas* it remarks gloomily, "The present dearth of genius and originality is attempted to be supplied with *splendid* editions of former writers"— this in May 1799, without any reference to the originality of *Lyrical Ballads.* The conservative *Gentleman's* perhaps leaned rather toward the taste and judgment side of the contemporary dual standard. It liked Bowles and Pye, and broke off quoting from William Sotheby's *The Battle of the Nile. A Poem*—in which it found "little to praise"—with an impatient "But enough of *sublimity, epithets,* and *repetitions!*" (April 1799). On the other hand, it approved of Landor's *Gebir* and pronounced the writer "a *poet*—who has caught the fire and imagery of Dante and Milton" (December 1799). Perhaps there is a reference to the novelty of the *Lyrical Ballads* implied in the comment on Mrs West's *Poems and Plays:*

At a time when the press swarms with publications pretending to be miscellaneous poems, but which are, in reality, ramifications of that dreadful system which threatens to pervert all our ideas of right and wrong; publications, whose least fault it is that they violate every known rule of composition; we ought surely to acknowledge our obligations to such authors as furnish us with safe and rational amusement. (October 1799, p. 881)

The ladies, if we can judge by the *Lady's Magazine or Entertaining Companion for the Fair Sex Appropriated Solely to their Use and Amusement*, were more sympathetic to the new poetry, although perhaps a little late in coming round. The 1797 volume contains, under the caption of "Poetical Essays," sonnets, odes, and prologues from current plays; it includes poems by the Laureate, Darwin, and Mrs. Radcliffe. There are "Inscriptions" identified as "From Mr. Southey's Poems." But in 1799 the journal reprints the influential essay on pastoral poetry from Drake's *Literary Hours*, and by 1800 Wordsworth has come into his own. "We Are Seven" was reprinted in April, "Lines Written near Richmond" in October, "The Complaint of a Forsaken Indian Woman" in December, and "The Female Vagrant" in the Supplement—all headed as from *Lyrical Ballads*. The next year saw "Lucy Gray" in April and "The Dungeon" in December. The first is identified as "By W. Wordsworth [From the Second Volume of 'Lyrical Ballads']"; the second—which, of course, is from Coleridge's *Osorio*—simply as "From the 'Lyrical Ballads'."

The rival *Lady's Monthly Museum or Polite Repository of Amusement and Instruction*, which a "Society of Ladies" began to publish in London in 1798, is rather delicate and elegant in tone—it provided in 1802 a portrait and sketch of William Hayley, labeling him "this elegant poet." They also were partial to pastorals for their poetry section, which rejoiced in the title of "The Apollonian Wreath," although generally they appeared to prefer the stilted sort:

> And now the plaintive bird of night
>   Sweetly warbles o'er the glade,
> And the sun's refulgent light
>   Sinks beneath the ev'ning shade.
>   (II, 161)

Or the kind of sentimentality reflected in "Lines, Occasioned by a Lady shedding tears at the scene in Pizarro, when Rollo is making his escape with Cora's Child, over the bridge, amidst the fire of soldiers." By 1800 someone does make fun, however, in "Ode on Contentment." Being entirely in the Modern Taste, where everything is described,—except the Subject proposed," which ends:

> Sound the trumpet, beat the drum;
> Tweedle-dee and tweedle-dum;
> Gird your armour cap-à-pee,
> Tweedle-dum and tweedle-dee
>   (IV, 237)

In May 1801 the editors printed Wordsworth's "Three years she grew," calling it "Lucy," and giving no credit. The big feature of that issue of the magazine, however, was Louisa, the Lady of the Haystack, complete with a portrait of the mad protegé of Hannah More, a poor girl who preferred to live under a haystack and who was rumored to be an illegitimate child of the Austrian emperor.

Other journals which provided no reviews nevertheless published verse, original and reprinted, in selections that served as a sort of barometer of poetic taste. Such a one was the *Universal Magazine of Knowledge and Pleasure.* In 1797 the pieces the editors chose were from the ubiquitous Laureate Pye, Prologues to plays, and the then flourishing sonnets. In 1798-1799 there began to appear—along with verses by Helen Maria Williams, Monk Lewis, Richard Polwhele, and W.L. Bowles—some ballads of Southey's and, in October 1799, "Goody Blake and Harry Gill," listed as "From Lyrical Ballads, &c." Less indicative of the poetic climate is the *Spirit of the Public Journals, Being an impartial selection of the most exquisite Essays and Jeux D'esprits, principally prose, that appear in the newspapers and other publications,* since, as its title suggests, it offered principally light entertainment. What verse it printed dealt largely in politics and parody. In 1798 its selections included a *Botany-Bay Eclogue* and Coleridge's "The Recantation: An Ode," but nothing from *Lyrical Ballads.*

Wordsworth fared a little better in the *Entertaining Magazine or Polite Repository of Elegant Amusement, containing Pleasing Extracts from Modern Authors. With Many original Pieces, and New Translations, in Prose and Verse.* This journal, which began publication in 1803, called its poetry section by the elegant name of "The Temple of Apollo." In its first year it reprinted poems by Robert Bloomfield, Landor, Charles Lloyd, Mrs. Robinson, Southey, Coleridge, Mrs. Opie—and two of Wordsworth's. The titles given the latter are interesting indications of tastes and emphases: "The Old Cumberland Beggar. A description," and "The Sad Story of Ruth."

Although Arthur Aikin's *Annual Review and History of Literature* did not begin publication until 1803, it looked back to the *Lyrical Ballads* and revealed the common critical duality. Thus James Grahame's *The Sabbath, and Sabbath Walks*—which had gone through three editions by 1805, and of which the *Literary Journal* declared "our author has hit upon the very soul of descriptive poetry, the particularizing of circumstances" (IV, 496)—is summed up by the *Annual Review* in the words "wants correctness" but "has true feeling" (IV, 591). It rejoiced that James Mercer's *Lyric Poems* had reached a second edition in 1804, because:

Here is an author, however, who, without either novel or obsolete expressions, compound words, inverted constructions, daring flights, or bold transitions, the snares of genius, and the refuge of dullness, at once delights and instructs, entertains the imagination, and touches the heart, by means of pure native English, pure native feeling, genuine taste and lively fancy. (III, 563)

From so much it is apparent that the *Annual Review* fancied itself as following the popular poetic golden mean, eschewing the excesses of Della Cruscanism on the one side and the Wordsworthian lowness on the other. When Wordsworth's *Poems in Two Volumes* came out in 1807, the *Annual* gave it (pp. 521-29) a "survey more detailed and laborious than our usual practice, or, in some respects, their importance, might seem to require," because they were "anxious to combat a system which appears to us so injurious to the author, and so dangerous to public taste." They went back to discuss the Preface to the *Lyrical Ballads* and to argue that the justification Wordsworth gives there for the use of meter might just as well be given to support the poetic diction he is attacking, and that his definition of a poet is inadequate because it omits "that kind of fancy, akin to wit, which 'glancing from heaven to earth, from earth to heaven' pervading, as it were, the whole world of nature and of art, snatches from each its beauteous images, combines, adapts, arranges them by a magic of its own, peoples with them its new creations, and at length pours forth in one striking, brilliant, yet harmonious whole." This kind of fancy is the "true parent" of poetic diction and no rationale could ever "deter the genuine poet from employing it; it is his native tongue." Therefore, the *Annual* critics conclude that:

it does appear to us somewhat ridiculous, not to say arrogant, in Mr. Wordsworth, to imagine that he has discovered anything, either in the trivial incidents which he usually makes the subjects of his narrations, or in the moral feelings and deductions which he endeavours to associate with them, too sublime for the admission of such decoration. (VI, 524)

Such as was used by Virgil and Milton! "Thus much for the system of Mr. Wordsworth, which appears to us a frigid and at the same time an extravagant one." By this tally, Wordsworth lacks both correctness and fancy; he is granted "a reflecting mind, and a feeling heart," but he is prosaic, prolix, and in "some parts absolutely mean."[6]

Southey's name, as we have already seen, was often associated with Wordsworth's—as he said many years later, "for honour & for dishonour";[7] the critical environment of *Lyrical Ballads* was inevitably influenced by this association. Southey appears to be the victim of what is essentially an attack upon Wordsworth's supposedly un-realistic portrayals of common people which was published in the *Literary Journal, a Review of Literature, Science, Manners and Politics.* The *Literary Journal* began publica-tion in 1803, and did not review *Lyrical Ballads* but delivered an indirect indictment in an 1805 critique of Southey's *Metrical Tales and other Poems:*

the opinion which he seems to entertain of the reach of his countrymen is little less degrading than that which is held forth by the author of "Goody Blake and Harry Gill." If *Tam o'Shanter,* and the other poems of Burns and Ramsay are adapted to the capacities of the common people of Scotland, and express their ideas and sentiments in their own language; and if the ballads and tales of Wordsworth and Southey do the same by the common people of England, what a mortifying comparison for the latter! . . . But, indeed, nothing can be more wide of the real sentiments of the common people than *every thing* that Mr. S. or Mr. Wordsworth, or Mr. Coleridge have written. There never was a countryman in Great Britain who uttered or dreamt of those *effusions of a gentle sensibility* on the horrors of war, the evils of the poor, the woes of marriage, and such other topics as are touched on in the tales before us. . . . We have heard a fine lady who never spoke to a countrywoman in her life, without a supercilious look, or a simper of condescension, admire beyond measure the *nature* that appeared in the "Idiot Boy" of Wordsworth, as she will probably do the tender *humanity* of Southey's "Battle of Blenheim." But an old Goody or Gaffer, whose language and sentiments are supposed to be here uttered, would, (and the trial has been made,) be unable to conceive such things could ever come out of the mouth of a human creature. (V, 159-60)

When the tables were turned, as is fair enough, Southey, Coleridge, and Wordsworth all basked in the praise. The *General Review of British and Foreign Literature* did not begin publication until 1806, rather late for a review of *Lyrical Ballads,* yet still expressed its views indirectly in the first volume though a long, favorable critique of Southey's *Madoc* that surveys recent literary history:

At this epoch so dangerous for our taste a Burns and a Cowper appeared; who had never used those swaddling clothes, but who moved and thought with much of Nature's genuine energy and freedom. These struck the first sparks of reformation. Southey, Wordsworth, and Coleridge then arose, determined to break the degrading charm that was imprisoning our real taste and feeling. They boldly appealed to Nature, and made simplicity their study as much as the other class pursued only art. The consequence has been a great improvement; a revivification of our poetical character.

It is true of these as of all reformers that they have sometimes gone into extremes. They have sometimes not only torn off the lace, but they have likewise rent the garment. In removing the cumbersome decorations of false taste, they have sometimes exposed the nudity of Nature. This, however, is an evil that will soon correct itself. Simplicity is a great ornament of true beauty, but it must not become slovenly and vulgar. Our charming countrywomen are now shewing us in their dress, that it is possible to combine the most impressive elegance with simplicity. . . . Let us be grateful for the good they have done, and the works they have produced, without looking *only* at their occasional defects. (I, 509-10)

Now Wordsworth is hailed as part of a great reformation toward Nature and simplicity, but something of the familiar critical balance remains: note that, as we shall see in more detail in the next chapter, the approved simplicity must be elegant.

Up until 1807 the *Lyrical Ballads* was the chief factor in establishing Wordsworth's reputation with the critics, since *An Evening Walk* and *Descriptive Sketches* had made little impression and were obviously superseded by a new style. After the publication in that year of Wordsworth's *Poems in Two Volumes*, the critics sensed a new game; but their judgments were still strongly conditioned by their views of *Lyrical Ballads*, and still constitute a part of that work's critical environment. For *Poems* seemed to some to confirm and clarify a "system" which Wordsworth had promulgated in the Preface to *Lyrical Ballads*. Nearly all reviewers agreed that *Poems* was not entirely satisfactory. Some thought the new work a sad decline from the success of *Lyrical Ballads*; others took it as abundant evidence that they were right in their first misgivings. The crux of the retrospective comment on *Lyrical Ballads* was whether they were unaffectedly simple, a welcome reform from the tinsel and glitter, having as Byron put it in his review in *Monthly Literary Recreations* (July 1807), "a native elegance, natural and uneffected." Or whether this simplicity had in it the seeds of "vulgarity, affectation, and silliness," as Jeffrey insisted in his *Edinburgh Review* scrutiny of *Poems* (October 1807). Both Byron and Jeffrey looked back at *Lyrical Ballads* with much favor. Byron said it had "not undeservedly met with a considerable share of public applause" and Jeffrey admitted it was "unquestionably popular; and . . . deservedly popular." Favorable also were the recollections of other critics. The *Eclectic Review's* commentator pointed out: "Mr. Wordsworth has distinguished himself, by his 'Lyrical Ballads,' as one of the boldest and most fortunate adventurers in the field of innovation" (January 1808). Even the vituperative writer in the *Critical Review*, who found *Poems* "a silly book" claimed his memory had "often dwelt with delight" on "Tintern Abbey," "Evening sail to Richmond," "Michael," and "a few more of the pieces contained in his first publication of Lyrical Ballads" (August 1807). It is noteworthy, however, that these are not among the most simple poems in the collection. Neither are those picked out by the *Eclectic Review* critic as the most successful pieces: "Old Cumberland Beggar," "Tintern Abbey" again, and "Verses on the Naming of Places." And these, the reviewer reminds the poet, are not in the "real language of men," but in "diction of transcendent beauty" (IV, 38).

Much of the animus of the reception of *Poems* and the retrospective comment on *Lyrical Ballads* came from the tendency in some quarters to lump Wordsworth, Southey, and Coleridge into a school and, as we have seen in the

General Review article, hail Wordsworth as a reformer of English poetry. Jeffrey explained that he had gone through *Poems* with such particular care just so that his readers could determine for themselves whether the author of such verses could be "entitled to claim the honours of an improver or restorer of our poetry" (*Edinburgh Review*, October 1807). Jeffrey, it seems, could not let go of *Lyrical Ballads*, for he has a great deal more to say about it a year later in his review of George Crabbe's *Poems* (April 1808). Here he discusses in some detail such characters as Matthew, Martha Ray, the owl imitator in "There was a boy," and Lucy—always attempting to show that they were not normal, common people, but rather idiosyncratic, unique specimens, fantastical and unnatural. "From these childish and absurd affectations," he pontificates, "we turn with pleasure to the manly sense and correct picturing of Mr. Crabbe."

This criterion of normality is the familiar correctness once again, and the persistence of the critical dualism is apparent in the reaction to *Poems in Two Volumes* by the *Cabinet or Monthly Report of Polite Literature*. This journal started up in 1807, and one of its first major reviews was of Wordsworth's *Poems*. Interestingly, the critic also considered the new collection as a decline from the successful simplicity of *Lyrical Ballads*: "By the merit of his first publication, he had nearly established a theory of poetical simplicity; but we are fearful that by the *de*merit of this he has overthrown it" (April 1808). Although the reviewer gives lip service to the emotional side of the critical spectrum, what the journal really stresses is correctness and propriety. Pratt, for instance, "always writes to the heart; and hence his productions have acquired their popularity"—but the characteristics of his muse are "suavity, simplicity, elegance, and tenderness" (July 1807), and the *Poetic Sketches* of T. Gent "merit the praise of correctness, simplicity, and sometimes elegance" (August 1807).

Clearly simplicity ought to be associated with elegance, and the reviewers get uneasy when it slips into "absurdities":

Mr. Wordsworth possesses several of the most essential qualities of the poet. He has a lively fancy, strong feelings, an imagination bold, and sometimes even sublime, an originality of expression, and has contemplated the scenery of nature for himself, but in taste he is deficient, and has still to learn 'the last and greatest art, the art to blot.' (*The Cabinet*, III, 249)

Many critics seemed to feel this need to restore the balance of the feeling-judgment standard. In the same way Jeffrey hailed the manly correctness of Crabbe, and the *British Critic* reviewer of *The Simpliciad* welcomed that satire as a new *Baviad*: even as Gifford had overcome the monster of Della Cruscanism, so a new hero had arisen to strike a blow "on the contrary side, to drive back the offenders, if possible, into the middle line of taste, judgment, and good sense" (February 1809).

Just how far Wordsworth's simplicity was off that happy middle line is the subject of the next chapter.

CHAPTER FOUR

Simplicity

and the *Lyrical Ballads*

Where Wordsworth stood on the current issue of "simplicity" was crucial to the critical acceptance of the *Lyrical Ballads* and still is to his position in English literary history. Havens thought that he outraged the critics by outdoing them: he took their own shibboleth and seemed to be parodying it. Danby, on the other hand, argues that Wordsworth's "simplicity" was deliberately achieved: it was sophisticated and complex, not really simple at all. Or, as Randall Jarrell put it, "It's so simple I can't understand it."[1] Certainly the truth of the matter is complicated and deserves some special attention.

When in 1808 *The Simpliciad* marked Wordsworth as "the founder of the simple school," it seemed to be taking most of its evidence from *Poems in Two Volumes*:

> Poets, who fix their visionary sight
> On Sparrow's eggs in prospect of delight,
> With fervent welcome greet the glow-worm's flame,
> Put it to bed and bless it by its name. . . .
> And dance with laughing daffodils. . . .
> Of apostolic daisies learn to think. . . .
> Whine over tatter'd cloaks and ragged breeches
> And moralize with gatherers of leeches.
>
> (94-113)

Included in the indictment, however is:

> Or measure muddy ponds from side to side,
> And find them three feet long and two feet wide—

thus indicating that "The Thorn" and *Lyrical Ballads* were
tarred with the same simple brush. From such remarks,
and especially from the title of the satire, one might get
the impression that simplicity itself is under attack. Not so.
Simplicity, we are definitely told,

> gives the charm to Raphael's chaste design,
> Bids Delphi's God with matchless beauty shine,
> And stamps with life "the tale of Troy devine"
>
> (21-3)

This favored Simplicity is not, however, the sort that is

> with rags defil'd
> A stammering, stagg'ring, puling, puny child:
> But the great mother of a noble race,
> Full-shaped, harmonious, firm in voice and pace,
> Inform'd by science, and array'd by grace.
>
> (24-8)

If we make a quick mental inventory of Raphael's
Madonnas, the Apollo of Belvedere, and Pope's translation
of Homer, we must become suspicious of just what this
critic meant by "simplicity." Although he did not sign his
work, he was probably Richard Mant, whose memoir
attached to his edition of *The Poetical Works* of Thomas
Warton, published in 1802 and thus closer to the *Lyrical
Ballads* in time than the satire, may help to define his terms.
He expresses his approval of Warton's popular "The
Suicide" for its appeal "not only to fancy, but to the heart,"
its "most striking poetical imagery" clothed in "the most
impressive diction" and "heightened by the tenderest sentiments," all of which conspired "to promote the noblest
purposes" (clii). His objections to the poem are more
illuminating: it has too much alliteration and is too allegorical, producing obscurity through the figurativeness of the

language—all unnecessary, since "a sentiment truly dignified does not want any pomp of language to support it."

Mant's approved simplicity, it thus appears, was dignified and sentimental—a connection characteristic of the
critics of a day when *simple*, as we have already had some
indication, was one of the most common critical epithets,
for praise or for blame, usually the former. Even Coleridge,
writing under the pseudonym of Nehemiah Higginbottom,
made fun of the popularity of the concept in his "Sonnets
Attempted in the Manner of Contemporary Writers." He
himself had been urged by Charles Lamb: "Cultivate
simplicity, Coleridge; or rather, I should say, banish
elaborateness; for simplicity springs spontaneous from the
heart, and carries into daylight its own modest buds, and
genuine, sweet, and clear flowers of expression" (letter,
November 8, 1796). Appropriately, Coleridge entitled
Sonnet II "To Simplicity," and enthused, "O! I do love
thee, meek *Simplicity*!" (*Monthly Magazine*, November
1797). Actually, however, as we see again and again,
simplicity was likely to be associated not so much with
meekness as with elegance, correctness, tenderness, and
pathos. Simplicity was of course a matter of both subject
and style, with different emphases for different commen-
tators. It was also frequently connected with the rustic and
the pastoral.

We might profitably review what some critics of the
Lyrical Ballads era had to say on the subject of simplicity.
The *Analytic Review*, for instance, declared that the
language of elegiac poetry shoule be "simple and affecting"
(November 1798), while the *Anti-Jacobin* thought the
"Irish Boy" was "simple" and "pathetic" (March 1799) and
the *Annual* remarked that all domestic subjects required
"pathos, simplicity, nature" (II [1804], 556). Likewise, the
Poetical Register for 1805 hailed Montgomery's "masculine
yet elegant simplicity (p. 485); the *Cabinet* approved

Pratt's "suavity, simplicity, and tenderness" (July 1807) and T. Gent's "correctness, simplicity, and sometimes elegance" (August 1807); and the *Gentleman's Magazine* hoped that Beattie's *Miscellanies* would lead to a restoration of "simplicity and correctness" (December 1799). The *Critical Review* in a 1797 comment on Coleridge's "Ode on the Departing Year" argued that simplicity "should for ever accompany the lyric muse" (XXI, 343), and later reported that Charlotte and Sophia King had been led by the splendour of epithets to deviate from "the path of simplicity" (March 1798); and the *General Review* on Southey's *Madoc* pontificated, "Simplicity is a great ornament of true beauty" (1806).

Nathan Drake, whose *Literary Hours* appeared first in the same year as the *Lyrical Ballads*, declared, as we recall, in his essay "On Pastoral Poetry" much reprinted in the journals of the day: "I am persuaded, however, that simplicity in diction and sentiment, a happy choice of rural imagery, such incidents and circumstances as may even *now* occur in the country, with interlocutors equally removed from vulgarity or considerable refinement, are all that are essential to success." In a note added to his 1800 edition, Drake remarked that Southey in his "English Eclogues" tried to do some of the things he suggested, and three of these poems Drake picked out as especially distinguished for their "Simplicity and beauty."

With the poets writing and being read at the turn of the century the attitude toward simplicity is similar to that among the critics. In *Table Talk*, published in 1782, Cowper had an influential Golden Age vision of the primitive simplicity of poetry:

> In Eden, ere yet innocence of heart
> Had faded, poetry was not an art;
> Language, above all teaching, or, if taught,
> Only by gratitude and glowing thought,

> Elegant as simplicity, and warm
> As ecstacy, unmanacled by form,
> Not prompted, as in our degen'rate days,
> By low ambition and the thirst of praise
>   (584-91).

Against this *artless* concept of "elegant as simplicity,"
place Pinkerton's *cultivated* view in "The Education of the
Muse," published the same year:

> And now the charms of fair design
> And elegance the Goddess can combine
> Like sweet simplicity:
> Her trains declared the cultivated mind.

Thomas Sanderson, whose *Original Poems* (published at
Carlisle in 1800, and written in Cumberland, Wordsworth's county) included "Simplicity; a Pastoral," thus
putting into practice Drake's advice. Similarly, the preface
to William Perfect's *Poetic Effusions; Pastoral, Moral,
Amatory, and Descriptive* (1796) declared that "above all"
pastoral poetry required "a simplicity of expression, which
is acknowledged to be the unstudied diction, the spontaneous offspring of nature." Matilda Betham's poem
entitled "To Simplicity" (*Elegies and Other Small Poems*
[1797]) hails the personification as "Fair village nymph."
In "Amwell: A Descriptive Poem" John Scott declares
that the "sweet simplicity" of rural life delights, and the
1782 edition of his *Poetical Works* is embellished with an
engraving of a female form—probably a muse—gracefuly
dropping a manuscript onto an altar labeled "Sacred to
Simplicity." In his "Ode, on May" (*Miscellaneous Pieces,
in Prose and Verse* [1793]), Charles Graham, who calls
himself "Writing Master and Teacher of the English Language," lauds the natural simplicity of primroses and
daisies:

> There's nought in the garden, tho' cultur'd with care
> Can with these in the charms of simplicity vie.

Much wider than this rural emphasis, and perhaps most genuinely simple of all, is the pugnacious defensiveness of Mrs. Hale's ending her *Poetical Attempts* (1800) with this address to all "Critics":

> Here I defy the proudest he
> To laugh at my simplicity.

Even the satirists of the day, however, agreed to praise simplicity, with or without tongue in cheek. Thomas James Mathias, probably author of the notorious *Pursuits of Literature*, declares in *The Imperial Epistle from Kien Long, Emperor of China, to George the Third, King of Great Britain* (1794)

> All pomp of words my sober years decline,
> Simplicity and truth illumine my line.

And in his *An Equestrian Epistle in Verse to the Rt. Hon. the Earl of Jersey* (1796) he modestly remarks, "Simplicity's my aim." In more serious vein, John Wolcot (the infamous Peter Pindar) wrote to Sir Christopher Hawkins about the poems of a miller's daughter whom he was offering to sponsor, as he had the painter Opie: "she seems to prefer things to words, substance to shadow, simplicity to affectation, in short a shirt without ruffles to ruffles without a shirt."[2]

Although William Mason's *English Garden* was written as early as 1772-1781, his popularity at the turn of the century is attested to by the *Monthly Magazine's* judgment in August 1797: "In our present gallery of the muses, which is not very splendidly furnished, the first place must be allotted to Mr. Mason." And his influential *Garden* begins:

> To thee, divine Simplicity! to thee,
> Best arbitress of what is good and fair.

Of course to the eighteenth century simplicity was quite literally divine, because it was revealed in "nature's simple plan." Newton himself had laid it down that "Nature is pleased with simplicity, and affects not the pomp of superfluous causes" (*Principia, III*). We therefore find Hannah More writing of "Simplicity divine" (*Florio*, 1786) and Mary ("Perdita") Robinson, of "the fairest daughter of the earth,/Divine SIMPLICITY! of humble birth." (*Modern Manners*, 1793). Simplicity also has a divine charm for Edwin, the hero of James Beattie's *The Minstrel*, who reminded Dorothy Wordsworth of her poet brother (*EY*, p. 101):

> Of late, with cumbersome, though pompous show
> Edwin would oft his flowery rhyme deface,
> Through ardour to adorn; but Nature now
> To his experienced eye a modest grace
> Presents, where Ornament the second place
> Holds, to intrinsic worth and just design
> Subservient still. Simplicity apace
> Tempers his rage: he owns her charm divine,
> And clears th' ambiguous phrase, and lops th' unwielding line.
>
> (II, lviii)

What is complicating and perplexing, is that Beattie's verse does not strike us as notably simple, and Perdita Robinson was one of the notoriously pretentious Della Cruscans! She even wrote an "Ode to Della Crusca," including these palpitating lines:

> Enlighten'd Patron of the sacred Lyre!
> Whose ever-varying, ever-witching song
>   Revibrates on the heart
>   With magic thrilling touch,
> Till ev'ry nerve, with quiv'ring throb divine,
> In Maddn'ing tumults, owns thy wondrous pow'r.

With some justice, the *Annual Review* dismissed her *Poetical Works* in 1807 as "unmeaning exaggeration and decorated inanity."

We wonder, therefore, about the true parentage of this "simplicity of humble birth," whose name is so often called upon by those who nevertheless seem scarcely to follow in her train. Charlotte Smith, whose *Elegiac Sonnets* went through twelve editions between 1784 and 1811, piously says in her preface; "I can hope for readers only among the few, who, to sensibility of heart, join simplicity of taste." She apparently got readers whose idea of simplicity included personifications and poetic diction of the sort shown in her "To Fancy," which begins:

> Thee, Queen of Shadows!—shall I still invoke,
> Still love the scenes thy sportive pencil drew,
> When on mine eyes the early radiance broke
> Which shew'd the beauteous rather than the true!
> Alas! long since those glowing tints are dead,
> And now 'tis thine in darkest hues to dress,
> The spot where pale Experience hangs her head
> O'er the sad grave of murder'd Happiness!

When Percival Stockdale wrote an introduction for the posthumous publication of Samuel Marsh Oram's *Poems* (1794), he took a very chip-on-the-shoulder attitude toward the reception of his untrained protegé: "I anticipate the sneer of presumptious ignorance, at the serious attention which I have given to the following productions, which are written with a remarkable simplicity of language; with a simplicity that is tricked out with no meretricious ornaments;— which was written by a youth who was not in an elevated rank of life; and who was unacquainted with what would have been useless to him, in *his* situation, the mean, and ostentatious arts of popularity." After all this protesting, the modern reader expects something slightly more simple than such poems as "Evening," which opens thus:

> From occidental skies the solar ray
> Fringes the fleecy clouds with golden hues;
> And rising o'er yon hill the moon persues,
> Through the immensity of space, her way.

We are also given a conventional sonnet to a nightingale—
"A pleasing melancholy o'er me steals"—and an "Ode;
Written near the Ruins of a Nobleman's Elegant Mansion,"
complete with a nymph and Flora!

One suspects that Hannah More was right when she
wrote in a Prefatory Letter to Mrs. Montagu attached to
her protegé Ann Yearsley's *Poems on Several Occasions*
(1785), "You will find her, like all unlettered Poets,
abounding in imagery, metaphor, and personification; her
faults, in this respect, being rather those of superfluity than
of want." It is worth noting that Mrs. Yearsley, who was
a Milkwoman, insisted on calling herself "Lactilla." So the
unlettered James Chambers, "Itinerant Poet," who claimed
to have only a month of schooling and who specialized
in acrostics—notably triple acrostics—usually shows a
literary and elegant style even in homey contexts. His
"Morning Winter Pieces. Written one Morning in a Cart-
shed, on the Author finding his Limbs covered with Snow,
blown through the Crevices," begins:

> What a striking scene's displayed
>   Winter with his freezing train,
> Verd'rous fields in White arrayed,
>   Snow-drop whiteness decks the plain.

The Bonny Irish Boy, the title-piece of an eight-page
poetical pamphlet published in 1799, may be considered
pathetically simple; but listen to the language of one of the
poems, "The Tempest":

> Cease, rude Boreas, blust'ring railer,
>   List ye landsmen all to me:
> Messmates, hear a brother sailor
>   Sing the dangers of the sea,
> From bounding billows, first in motion,
>   When the distant whirlwinds rise,
> To the tempest-troubled ocean,
>   And seas contend with skies.

This in a very cheaply printed collection, on sleazy paper, aimed at a popular audience, selling for not over a penny and possibly half-penny, demonstrates possible incongruities of the prevalent alliance between simplicity and elegance.

To professors of this rather confused worship of simplicity, Wordsworth understandably seemed the prophet of a new and fanatical sect. Although some of the critics of *Lyrical Ballads*, like those writing in the *Analytical Review* and the *New Annual Register*, spoke favorably of a genuine simplicity, the complaint of fashionable excess soon sounded. *The Monthly Mirror* comment on the 1800 edition complained that "an obscurity too often arises, from a romantic search after simplicity" (June 1801). Coleridge, of course, blamed the Preface: "if it had not been for the *Preface*" the critics "would themselves have never dreamt of affected Simplicity & Meanness of Thought & Diction." This comment is not without irony, since Coleridge appears to have been largely responsible for the idea of the Preface; certainly Wordsworth blamed him for it.[3] At any rate, by 1801 the *Monthly Mirror* was pointing the finger at a "new school" in its review of Joseph Cottle's *Alfred, an Epic Poem:* "With respect to style, it may be observed, generally, that Mr. Cottle sometimes creeps where he should soar; that, in aiming at simplicity, he often descends to meanness and imbecility . . . from the influence of a false taste, contracted by an admiration of the new school" (XI, 396). By the appearance of Wordsworth's *Poems* (1807) the line had hardened against the simple system. A reviewer in *Le Beau Mode* declared, "We hoped that the childish effusions that were mixed among the poems of the former work [*Lyrical Ballads*], were the errors of a mind then in its poetical dawn," but *Poems* demonstrated that "Mr. Wordsworth has ruined himself by his affectation of simplicity" (II, 138, 142). By *Peter Bell* (1819) the *Edinburgh Monthly Review* spoke positively of a "puerile affectation of simplicity": "We say, unhesitatingly, affectation because we are perfectly convinced that no one of the rank and education of a gentleman, could or would employ the ideas and expressions to which we allude, without a conscious effort to do so" (II, 659).

As Jeffrey put it in his 1802 review of Southey's *Thalaba*:

The followers of simplicity are, therefore, at all times in danger of occasional degradation; but the simplicity of this new school seems intended to insure it. *Their* simplicity does not consist, by any means, in the rejection of glaring or superfluous ornament,—in the substitution of elegance to splendour, or in the refinement of art which seeks concealment in its own perfection. It consists, on the contrary, in a very great degree, in the positive and *bona fide* rejection of art altogether, and in the bold use of those rude and negligent expressions, which would be banished by a little discrimination. One of their own authors, indeed, has very ingeniously set forth (in a kind of manifesto that preceded one of their most flagrant acts of hostility), that it was their capital object "to adapt to the uses of poetry, the ordinary language of conversation among the middling and lower orders of the people."

Despite his quotation marks, Jeffrey appears to be paraphrasing here the Advertisement to the 1798 edition of the *Lyrical Ballads*: "experiments . . . written chiefly with a view to ascertain how far the language of conversation in the middle and lower classes of society is adapted to the purposes of poetic pleasure." It suited his purposes to ignore Wordsworth's significant revision in the Preface of the key phrase to "a selection of the real language of men in a state of vivid sensation."

Although Jeffrey appears to recognize an elegant, artistic simplicity, his objection to Wordsworth's practice reflects a common antithesis between simplicity and art. George Davies Harley, in his crude *Ballad Stories, Sonnets &c.*

(1799), takes credit for being "unstudy'd in the schools,/ Where simple Nature yields to specious art":

> *I* cannot write by wary judgment's rules,
> But risk the *head*, to gratify the *heart*.
>
> (p. 106)

The real crux of the matter, of course, is Jeffrey's overlooking Wordsworth's *selection*. Wordsworth was by no means rejecting art, as Jeffrey charged. Indeed, his formulation actually reflected much of the contemporary aesthetic. In a passage added to the Preface in 1802, but perhaps influenced by a *Monthly Magazine* article on "Is Verse Essential to Poetry?" (July 1796),[4] he repeats many of the accepted critical tags: "this selection, wherever it is made with true taste and feeling, will of itself form a distinction far greater than would at first be imagined, and will entirely separate the composition from the vulgarity and meanness of ordinary life . . . for, if the Poet's subject be judiciously chosen, it will naturally, and upon fit occasion, lead him to passions the language of which, if selected truly and judiciously, must necessarily be dignified and variegated, and alive with metaphors and figures" (*PW*, II, 392; *Prose Wks.*, I, 137). There we have the *true taste and feeling, passion, dignified and variegated* with which Jeffrey himself must have agreed. Of course, much of the difference between Wordsworth and Jeffrey, as well as other caustic critics, was partly in the practice—*were* the subjects and the language "judiciously chosen"? The poet himself admitted he might have been guilty of personal associations which gave things "a false importance" and led him to write on "unworthy subjects" or use language based on "arbitrary connections of feelings and ideas with particular words and phrases" (*Prose Wks.*, I, 152, 153). But that is not all there is to the problem. Wordsworth's view of simplicity was not what Jeffrey ascribed to him, but it was not exactly the accepted one of the time either.

First, it is noteworthy that Wordsworth does not himself use the terms "simple" or "simplicity" in the early section of the Preface just quoted. He does not really place much emphasis on the honored shibboleth. In his well-known summation of his principal objects in *Lyrical Ballads* he says he intended to choose incidents and situations "from common life" and treat them in the "language really used by men." He does not touch the magic term until what is virtually an aside, a sort of gloss on "common life" (I quote from the 1800 version):

Low and rustic life was generally chosen because in that situation the essential passions of the heart find a better soil in which they can attain their maturity, are less under restraint, and speak a plainer and more emphatic language; because in that situation our elementary feelings exist in a state of greater simplicity and consequently may be more accurately contemplated, and more forcibly communicated; because the manners of rural life germinate from those elementary feelings; and from the necessary character of rural occupations are more easily comprehended; and are more durable; and lastly, because in that situation the passions of men are incorporated with the beautiful and permanent forms of nature. The language too of these men is adopted (purified indeed from what appear to be its real defects, from all lasting and rational causes of dislike or disgust) because such men hourly communicate with the best objects from which the best part of language is originally derived; and because, from their rank in society and the sameness and narrow circle of their intercourse, being less under the action of social vanity they convey their feelings and notions in simple and unelaborated expressions (*Prose Wks.*, I, 124; *cf. PW*, II, 386-7)

Wordsworth is here invoking simplicity of both subject and style, viewing both favorably. He recognizes some qualification later:

poems are extant, written upon more humble subjects, and in a more naked and simple style than what I have aimed at, which poems have continued to give pleasure from generation to generation. Now, if nakedness and simplicity be a defect, the fact here mentioned affords a strong presumption that poems somewhat less naked and simple are capable of affording pleasure at the present day; and all that I am now attempting is [1850: what I wished *chiefly* to attempt, at present, was] to justify myself for having written under the impression of this belief. (*Prose Wks.*, I, 144-6; *cf. PW*, II, 399)

This passage seems to admit that extreme simplicity can be a defect. Still later Wordsworth condemns as "trivial and simple" Dr. Johnson's little verse:

> I put my hat upon my head
> And walked into the Strand,
> And there I met another man
> Whose hat was in his hand.

From all this it appears that Wordsworth takes a partly pragmatic attitude towards simplicity—favoring that degree of simplicity which experience has proved to be acceptable; but, he would argue, acceptable because it is fundamental. Although his use of the concept is different from that of most contemporaries, there were some sympathetic vibrations.

M. Holford, for example, published in 1798 *Gresford Vale and Other Poems*, including among the latter "Rural Pleasures," which hailed a life "Far from the scenes of noisy strife," and asserted

> For pure delight and pleasure free
> Are gifts of thine, Simplicity.

I think Wordsworth would have agreed about the pleasure-giving pure and free. He also had a fellow-feeling with Thomas Dermody, who mourns in a Postscript to "The Retrospect" (published in *Poems, Moral and Descriptive* in 1800, but written some five years earlier): "I am sorry to imagine that the disesteem into which DESCRIPTIVE POESY has fallen, may have been caused by that neglect of simplicity in diction, and plan, which so shamefully marks the flimsy effusions of the present day." He himself professes to eschew "dazzling figures, metaphoric phrase and metaphysical scruple," proudly proclaiming: "I have ventured to use plain, unadulterated language, forcible expression, clear concise sentiment, and the unfashionable science of moral observation." Near the beginning of the Preface Wordsworth declared for poetry "well adapted to interest mankind permanently, and not unimportant in the quality, and in the multiplicity of its moral relations." Surely he put plain language primarily to the service of forcible expression of moral observations throughout *Lyrical Ballads*:

pride,/ . . . Is littleness ("Lines Left Upon a Seat in a Yew Tree")

> the gratitude of men
Has oftner left me mourning ("Simon Lee")

Could I but teach the hundredth part
Of what from thee I learn ("Anecdote for Fathers")

Have I not reason to lament
What man has made of man? ("Lines Written in Early Spring")

We murder to dissect ("The Tables Turned")

This is observation of moral simplicity, a fundamentalism built upon the human essentials of childhood and old age, pride and greed, poverty and idiocy.

In April 1801 Wordsworth wrote to Miss Taylor, who had applied the popular term to his works: "You flatter me, Madam, that my style is distinguished by a genuine simplicity. Whatever merit I may have in this way I have attained solely by endeavouring to look, as I have said in my preface, steadily at my subject" (*EY*, p. 328). Thus acceptable "simplicity" gets converted to "reality." What Wordsworth does is deny the trivially simple, but value the *essentially* simple. Most of the contemporary critics used the term, it is worth noting, in a largely negative context: the simple might be the natural, but it was primarily the *un*adorned and *un*sophisticated, the splendid pruned down to the elegant. As Charles Lamb told Coleridge, cultivating simplicity meant banishing elaborateness. Hugh Blair had established this "elegant simplicity" (Lecture xix). To Wordsworth, in so far as the concept was important, it had a positive value—the permanent, the real, the durable, the essential. His favorite critical terms were "elemental" and "eternal."

In a passage probably written in 1798, which later became part of the first book of *The Excursion*, Wordsworth said:

> much did he see of men,
> Their manners, their enjoyments, and pursuits,
> Their passions and their feelings; chiefly those
> Essential and eternal in the heart,
> That, 'mid the simpler forms of rural life,
> Exist more simple in their elements
> And speak a plainer language
> (341-7) [*cf.* MS B, 60-66
> (*PW*, V, 380-1); *The Pedlar*, 238-45]

The valued simple is "essential and eternal in the heart." A section of the Preface dropped in 1845 declares that the purposes of the *Lyrical Ballads* include "to follow the fluxes and refluxes of the mind when agitated by the great and simple affections of our nature" (*Prose Wks.*, I, 126). and says that the authors intended in part to sketch "characters of which the elements are simple, belonging rather to nature than to manners." The highest simplicity, therefore, is great and natural.

Thus the simple was for Wordsworth not, as Jeffrey complained and the *General Review* (I, 509) applauded, a repudiation of art, but rather the quintessence of art—removing, as Pater put it, the "superfluage" and getting to the real—"the real language of man" and the "essential passions of the heart." That is why Coleridge's suggestion of changing the phrase to "ordinary language," although logical enough in a way, was not acceptable.

It is accurate to say, as the *British Critic* did (XIV, 365), that Wordsworth was trying to recall English poetry "to simplicity and nature," only if these terms are understood to combine into the natural, elemental reality—which can never be simple in the sense of trivial or insignificant. In fact, it could even be magnificent! In the 1815 "Essay, Supplementary to the Preface," when Wordsworth had well passed the experimental stage of *Lyrical Ballads*, he still held up the great simplicity in these terms: "In the higher poetry, an enlightened Critic chiefly looks for a reflection of the wisdom of the heart and the grandeur of the imagination. Wherever these appear, simplicity accompanies them; Magnificence herself when legitimate, depending upon a simplicity of her own, to regulate her ornaments" (*PW*, II, 411; *Prose Wks.*, III, 64). There is, therefore, more truth than the reviewer of *Poems* in *The Satirist* realized in his comment: "Fond as he is of the words *nature, modesty, simplicity*, &c, this author perpetually betrays the most magnificent opinions of his own powers" (I, 189). Wordsworth was not excessively fond of the words "modesty" and "simplicity," but his kind of simplicity is important and worthy of the highest poetical powers. This view Blair had also authorized. Of the four kinds of simplicity he described, the last "stands opposed not to Ornament, but to Affectation of Ornament" and is in fact "compatible with the highest ornament": Homer "possesses this Simplicity in the greatest perfection" (Lecture xix).

One of the most interesting and revealing of Wordsworth's comments on simplicity comes in a letter of June 14, 1802, to his sister-in-law Sara Hutchinson about "Resolution and Independence": "the figure," he says, "presented in the most naked simplicity possible," provided a "feeling of spirituality or supernaturalness" (*EY*, p. 366). Obviously it is not enough to think of the simple as natural—the elementally simple is spiritual, *super*natural.

Wordsworth's well-known "recollection in tranquility" was a means of getting at this elemental simplicity, which was the core of that inevitability he chiefly valued. As Matthew Arnold remembered, Wordsworth called Goethe's poetry "not inevitable enough":[5] and all his comments on the German poet, whose works he did not know very well, indicate that he meant universal, fundamental. Wordsworth's criterion of inevitability is something like that of another German, Schelling, who put it thus: "In every period, therefore, we observe that the true artists are silent, simple, great and necessary in their manner—like Nature."[6]

There is, of course, a sense in which the universal is comprehensive and complicated, as it is in the works of Shakespeare, Wordsworth's favorite example. But there is another sense in which it is elementally simple, as in Wordsworth's example of the "Babes in the Wood":

> These pretty Babes with hand in hand
> Went wandering up and down;
> But never more they saw the Man
> Approaching from the Town.

Wordsworth does not bother to explain why he thinks these lines are admirable—just that by comparison Dr. Johnson's verse about the two men and their hats is "contemptible," and that the difference is not in the language but in the subject matter.

If one scene is any more from "common life" than the other, the advantage would seem to go to Dr. Johnson's men with the hats. What is superior about the "Babes in the Wood" is its basic appeal to essential human feelings, the fundamental universality of childish innocence and naivete. The feeling is simply elemental and permanent, as it is in "The Thorn," and "The Idiot Boy," and "A Forsaken Indian Woman"—indeed in most of Wordsworth's *Lyrical*

Ballads. And he is willing to use the language he thought appropriate to this subject matter, the "real language," with almost complete consistency.

Thus by revaluing and reconstituting the current standard of simplicity—or at least pushing it back in the direction of Blair's fourth kind of simplicity—Wordsworth was not merely trying to avoid "false refinements." He was seeking a unified aesthetic, a oneness of style and subject by which, as De Quincey put it later (crediting Wordsworth with the idea) style was not the dress but the incarnation of the subject[7]—real life in real language. Therefore Wordsworth came up against the contemporary duality of feeling versus correctness, and seemed to throw out the correctness side of the criterion—because he had a different concept of correctness. To him it was equated not with elegance, even with the elegance of simplicity, but with propriety in the sense of that which seemed to the poet inevitable because it fit into the essential humanity of the situation, and was therefore truly and fundamentally simple.

CHAPTER FIVE

Lyrical Ballads and
Innovation

How much of an "experiment" did Wordsworth and Coleridge present the literary world? Since Cottle and Arch launched the small volume, critical schools have waxed and waned, and literary history has been constantly reinterpreted in the light of newly discovered facts and newly developed theories; it is still hard to know where to have the *Lyrical Ballads*. The year of the first edition, 1798, has been canonized and memorized as a literary landmark, even—according to one critical cliché—the beginning of the English romantic movement. And clichés are not to be dismissed lightly, including the hoary "where there's smoke there's fire." But critics do not even agree on the essential character of romanticism, and most recognize that in any event it did not actually begin at a given time and in a specific document—unless, as has been suggested, with the serpent's addresses to Eve in the Garden of Eden: the first inciting against the established order. What did happen in 1798?

One of the earliest retrospective surveys seemed to think not very much. In October 1829 Francis Jeffrey closed a review of Mrs. Hemans' poems with this look back over his influential critical career as editor of the *Edinburgh Review:*

The tuneful quartos of Southey are already little better than lumber:—and the rich melodies of Keats and Shelley,—and the fantastical emphasis of Wordsworth,—and the plebeian pathos of Crabbe, are melting fast from the field of our vision. The novels of Scott have put out his poetry. Even the splendid strains of Moore are fading into distance and dimness, except where they have been married to immortal music; and the blazing star of Byron himself is receding from its place of pride. . . . The two who have the longest withstood this rapid withering of the laurel, and with the least marks of decay on their branches, are Rogers and Campbell; neither of them, it may be remarked, voluminous writers, and both distinguished rather for the fine taste and consummate elegance of their writings, than for that fiery passion, and disdainful vehemence, which seemed for a time to be so much more in favour with the public.

"Fantastical emphasis" may recognize novelty, but certainly does not give it much importance; and there is a *caput mortuum* tone to the whole recital. As we have seen (Chapter Three), as early as 1806 the *General Review and Foreign Literature* had called Southey, Wordsworth, and Coleridge "reformers," although in the tradition of Burns and Cowper. And Jeffrey in 1807 had objected to the claim that Wordsworth was "an improver and restorer of our poetry." Even thought the very objection suggests that the idea had some acceptance, the notion that something radically, significantly, and permanently different had happened with the publication of the *Lyrical Ballads* has come down to posterity most clearly from William Hazlitt's *Spirit of the Age* (1825):

the author of the *Lyrical Ballads* . . . has described all these objects in a way and with an intensity of feeling that no one else had done before him, and has given a new view or aspect of nature. He is in this sense the most original poet now living, and the one whose writings could the least be spared: for they have no substitute elsewhere. (Howe, XI, 89)

The distortions of time were exaggerating the novelty of the *Lyrical Ballads* by 1882 when the incredibly prolific Margaret Oliphant published her pioneering *The Literary*

History of England in the End of the Eighteenth and Beginning of the Nineteenth Century. With fine excess she insisted, "A shout of derision rose from all the critics; and England in general can scarcely be said to have been less than personally offended by this serious and almost solemn attempt to impose a new poetical creed upon her" (I, 278). Following in her train, early twentieth-century critics seem to have taken for granted the originality and monumental significance of the *Lyrical Ballads.* Oliver Elton, for example, declared "there had been nothing of the sort before"; and Elsie Smith, despite the fact that she had before her the evidence of the reviewers cited in her *An Estimate of William Wordsworth by His Contemporaries,* could still say that the 1798 volume "marked a complete change from anything that had appeared before."[1]

It remained for Robert Mayo, as late as 1954, to insist on "The Contemporaneity of the *Lyrical Ballads,*" to point out that the change was not so complete, since anticipation of Wordsworth's form and matter could be found in the periodical verse of the day, and that most of the reviewers were not hostile, but indeed "seemed to feel that the collection was not greatly out of line with contemporary practice."[2] Despite Mayo's valiant and generally influential efforts, however, we still find Margaret Drabble saying in 1966, "The poems in this one small volume were a revolution in poetry; they were completely new. . . . They were different in language, in intention, and in subject matter."[3]

Certainly "completely new" would need some qualification, but we cannot escape the feeling that there *is* considerable novelty here. Mayo himself does not deny it, although he is disposed to think the chief originality is in the poetic excellence, the superior treatment of themes and forms already familiar in the periodical press. Other critics who accept Mayo's basic view of the contemporaneity of the collection still look for aspects of originality in the quality of this excellence. Stephen Parrish seems to see it largely in a more dramatic handling of ballad elements, Charles Ryskamp in a greater psychological subtlety of Wordsworth's implicative use of narrative.[4] Let us look a little more at the novelty of the *Lyrical Ballads*, considering here not whether it actually was new and how, but the prior question of whether it was so regarded and in what context.

First, it is surely worth noting that Wordsworth himself stressed the unusual character of the book. Mayo makes the point that Coleridge, writing some seventeen years later in *Biographia Literaria*, argued that the *Lyrical Ballads* were not "in *themselves*" the cause of "this fiction of a *new school* of poetry," and that the omission of less than 100 lines from the two-volume 1800 edition would have defused nine-tenths of the criticism of the work—provided the reader had taken up the book as he would have "any other collection of poems" intermingling ordinary life with higher meditations—implying that a reader not prejudiced might possibly have looked at this as at any other collection.[5] But this argument is a product of Coleridge's later conservative years, when he had long since "snapped [his] squeaking baby-trumpet of Sedition" (*Letters*, I, 397) and did not wish to be associated with anything revolutionary. For, as Wordsworth's biographer and nephew, Christopher Wordsworth, later Bishop of Lincoln, put it in his remarks on the *Lyrical Ballads* in the official *Memoirs*, there was a suspicion that:

The clue to his *poetical* theory, in some of its questionable details, may be found in his *political* principles; these had been democratical, and still, though in some degree modified, they were of a republican character. At this period he entertained little reverence for ancient institutions, as such; and he felt little sympathy with the higher classes of society ([London, 1851], I, 125).

Whatever Coleridge thought, Wordsworth surely went out of his way to say that there was something different about the collection. In the "Advertisement"[6] Wordsworth insisted, "The majority of the following poems are to be considered as experiments." And it is significant that in the *Biographia Literaria* (Chap. XIV) Coleridge said that Wordsworth "presented" the poems as experiments, implying that he himself would not have done so, but making his friend's intention clear. Wordsworth was using the psychology well known today—especially in academic circles—that almost any departure can be justified as "an experiment." He tried to disarm his critics by admitting in the "Advertisement" that "readers accustomed to the gaudiness and inane phraseology of many modern writers . . . will look round for poetry, and will be induced to enquire by what species of courtesy these attempts can be permitted to assume that title." Sure enough, Dr. Burney in *The Monthly Review* "cannot regard them as *poetry*" (June 1799), and the painter Joseph Farington recorded in his *Diary* on June 17, 1806 (when the evidence for Wordsworth was still the *Lyrical Ballads*), that John Taylor had told him that Jerningham had told him that the Bishop of London had said of Wordsworth, Coleridge, and Southey: "Whatever merit there might be in them it was not *legitimate Poetry*" (ed. James Greig [London, 1924], III, 249). Wordsworth does go on to say that "the more conversant the reader is with our elder writers, and with those in modern times who have been the most successful in painting manners and passions, the fewer complaints of this kind will he have to make," suggesting that he actually is returning to older practice, and has some modern company. But he does not seem himself conscious of much contemporaneity.

In the 1800 Preface Wordsworth repeated the "what species of courtesy" gambit, and referred flatly to the contents as "Poems so materially different from those, upon which general approbation is at present bestowed" (*Prose Wks.*, I, 120; *PW*, II, 385). So convinced was he of this difference that on December 18, 1800, he added a postscript he considered of "great importance" to a letter to his new publishers, Longman and Rees, suggesting the advisability of sending copies of the second edition accompanied by an explanatory letter to a few eminent persons in an effort to help the sales, because "The Lyrical Ballads are written upon a theory professedly new, and on principles which many persons will be unwilling to admit." In a letter of June 1801 to his brother Richard, William had pleasure in reporting that "the reputation of the L.B. is spreading every day, though slowly, as might be expected from a work so original."[7]

We get the same picture from Dorothy, who was undoubtedly echoing her brother's opinions in her September 10, 1800, letter to Jane Marshall about the publication of the second edition:

The first volume sold much better than we expected, and was liked by a much greater number of people, not that we ever had much doubt of its finally making its way, but we knew that poems so different from what have in general become popular immediately after their publication were not likely to be admired all at once. The first volume I have no doubt has prepared a number of purchasers for the second, and independent of that, I think the second is much more likely to please the generality of readers. (*EY*, pp. 297-8)

Clearly, then, Wordsworth emphasized to himself, his readers, his publisher, and his family the differences of the *Lyrical Ballads*—particularly the first volume—from the poetry then popular. These claims of novelty seem also to have been accepted practically at face value by the reviewers. It is true, as Mayo pointed out, that the reviewers do not expatiate upon an amazing *nova stella* in the poetic firmament. But they usually begin with Wordsworth's statement that the *Lyrical Ballads* are to be considered an "experiment," and as far as I know nobody protests that this sort of thing has been going on all along and they do not see what the fuss is about. The *British Critic* pronounced the experiment a success, the *Critical Review* and the *New London Review* a failure; the *Monthly Mirror* wished the "style were more generally adopted." And, as we have seen, there was a tendency of the reviews of the 1807 *Poems in Two Volumes* to look back upon the *Lyrical Ballads* as a novel production, for good or bad. The *Cabinet* thinks it "had nearly established a theory of poetical simplicity" and the *Annual Review* now recognizes and deplores a "system and practice of poetry . . . both so entirely his own." The *Edinburgh Review* also looked back at the "strong spirit of originality" in the *Lyrical Ballads*, the "alarming innovation" which they had opposed and now felt entirely justified in having done so by *Poems'* confirmation of Wordsworth's "new school of poetry." Somewhat more favorably inclined, the *Eclectic Review*, in a critique written by James Montgomery, remembered, "In the age of poetical experiment, Mr. Wordsworth has distinguished himself, by his 'Lyrical Ballads,' as one of the boldest and most fortunate adventurers in the field of innovation."[8] The unfavorable view of the "novelty" is strongly expressed by *The Satirist, or Monthly Monitor*:

This gentleman published two volumes of Lyric [*sic*] Ballads some years ago, which were composed on a system of his own: as if poetry was a mechanical art, and performed its operations by certain regulated processes, and not an appeal to the hearts and feelings of mankind. Of this grand system of poetry, which was thus first discovered by Mr. Wordsworth, about the year of our Lord 1800, and was of course altogether unknown to Homer, Virgil, Shakespeare, Milton, and Dryden, the grand principle was, that nature could only be represented with fidelity by a close imitation of the language, and a constant adoption of the phrases, made use of by persons in the lowest stages of life: as if language were not entirely factitious and arbitrary; as if men of all ranks and situations were not the creatures of habit; as if the expressions of the meanest individuals were not the result of the education which they receive, while those of the higher orders are rendered natural by long usage to the well-informed and accomplished part of mankind. (I [November 1807], 188-189)

Another indicator of the feeling that something innovative had happened with the *Lyrical Ballads* is in the reaction of young men just coming to an awareness of poetry. Coleridge says in the *Biographia Literaria* that Wordsworth's admirers were found "chiefly among young men of strong sensibility and meditative minds; and their admiration (inflamed perhaps in some degree by opposition) was distinguished by its intensity, I might almost say, by its *religious* fervor" (II, 7). Coleridge was probably thinking of people like Hazlitt, De Quincey and John Wilson (later "Christopher North"). Hazlitt in his "My First Acquaintance with Poets" looks back to 1798 when he, just turned twenty, met Wordsworth and heard him read some of the poems which were to be in *Lyrical Ballads*: "the sense of a new style and a new spirit in poetry came over me. It had to me something of the effect that arises from the turning up of the fresh soil, or of the first welcome breath of Spring" (Howe, XVII, 117).

In 1803 De Quincey made a most curious advance to Wordsworth, writing him, "From the time when I first saw the 'Lyrical Ballads' I made a resolution to obtain (if I could) the friendship of their author." That was apparently in 1799, when De Quincey was only fourteen. He reviewed his early feelings in "Literary Novitiate," an 1837 essay about his experiences in 1801 among the Liverpool literary circle of Roscoe, Currie, and Shepherd: "to me, who . . . already knew of a grand renovation of poetic power—of a new birth in poetry, interesting not so much to England as to the human mind—it was secretly amusing to contrast the little artificial usages of their petty traditional knack with the natural forms of a divine art." No matter how much of this may have been a product of 1837 afterthoughts, there is still the 1803 letter of the humbly bold

young man. From Professor Jardine's College, Glasgow,
young John Wilson wrote on May 24, 1802, a similar but
more assured letter to Wordsworth, as a poet to whom
mankind was indebted for "the real feelings of human
nature, expressed in simple and forcible language." John
Hamilton Reynolds came, of course, later—he was only
four years old in 1798. But, despite his subsequent parody
of *Peter Bell*, he grew up in almost religious admiration of
Wordsworth, so that he wrote Benjamin Haydon (September 28, 1816): "when I think of the sun-like genius, & fine
firm principle of that Noble Poet;—I think higher of human
nature, of the age in which I live."[9]

In a way Wordsworth's protestations of unpopular
novelty seem perverse, because as we have seen the
Lyrical Ballads were published to make money—the only
reason Wordsworth could bring himself to release most of
his early works. It would have seemed more sensible for
him to have tried to smooth over the differences and stress
the similarities with the poetry people were then reading
and buying—to claim the spice of originality, perhaps, but
not material and unwelcome difference. Either Wordsworth genuinely believed in the great novelty of his volume
or he overemphasized the differences between this collection and most contemporary poetry as a defensive maneu-
ver to account for a feared poor reception—"the first
volume sold much better than we expected," said Dorothy.
Wordsworth always had an ambivalent democratic faith in
the "people" and an elitist distrust of the "public"—a
distinction he elaborated in "Essay Suplementary to the
Preface" in 1815, but which crops up in a letter on *Peter
Bell* in 1808.[10]

The *Lyrical Ballads* did, however, turn out to be something of a popular success, despite a good deal of folklore
to the contrary. As we have see, some of the reviews
were favorable, and most found something good to say.
The 1798 edition went slowly but did sell out by the spring

of 1800—R.S. Woof thinks because of the "vigorous advertisements" in Daniel Stuart's newspapers[11]—so that Longman ventured a new, enlarged edition that year. The collection went on to see a total of four British and one American editions in seven years, and undoubtedly would have been brought out again if it had not been merged into Wordsworth's *Works* in 1815. To get some adequate gauge of the extent of this popularity, however, we need to put it in the perspective of the demand for other contemporary poetry.

Perhaps we could expect avid sales of satires, especially of mysteriously anonymous work such as James Mathias' *The Pursuits of Literature*, which between 1794 and 1797 grew to four parts and by 1801 had seen eleven editions. William Gifford's *The Baviad* sold six editions from 1791 to 1800, and John Wolcot (Peter Pindar) needed four editions of *Tales of the Hoy* in one year—1798. But even the rather insipid William Hayley saw his *Triumphs of Temper* go through twelve editions from 1781 to 1803; and in September 1807 the *Cabinet* called him "one of the best (perhaps the very best) of our living poets" (I, 65)—although this was not by then the general critical opinion. Robert Bloomfield's *The Farmer's Boy* required five editions in two years (1800-01) and was translated into Latin in 1804. Of course Walter Scott's popular *The Lay of the Last Minstrel* turned up eight editions between 1805 and 1808. A number of more obscure authors also enjoyed considerable measures of popularity. Samuel Jackson Pratt's *Sympathy* made ten editions from 1781 to 1806. Three editions of P.L. Courtier's *Pleasures of Solitude* were issued in 1803-4. Although William Crowe's *Lewesdon Hill* took two editions the first year, 1788, another was not required until 1804—but then the *Poetical Register* remarked, "The merit of 'Lewesdon Hill' is so well known that it is unnecessary to say anything upon the subject." When in 1805 a second

edition of *The Sabbath* by James Grahame appeared, a
year after the first, the *Literary Journal* hailed the event as
"proof that whenever real traits of genius are exhibited the
public favor is ever ready to cherish them." And when the
third edition of William Smyth's *English Lyrics* came out in
1806 the *Poetical Register* declared, "It is difficult to
account for the circumstance of these English lyrics having
passed through only three editions in nine years."[12] By
these standards it would appear that the *Lyrical Ballads*
were not a phenomenal but a reasonable success.

Furthermore, as Mayo has well pointed out, much of the
verse of the time, including Wordsworth's, achieved a wide
circulation in magazines, most of which had poetry sec-
tions they were free to fill by pilfering from current
volumes of verse. Wordsworth's poems did not appear in
the conservative *Gentleman's Magazine*, and they were
probably not in as much general demand as were Southey's
ballads and the productions of the Laureate, Henry James
Pye. By Mayo's count, there were between 1798 and 1802
twenty-three reprintings of fifteen different poems from the
Lyrical Ballads. This fact does not, indeed, indicate any
special distinction; the *Universal Magazine*, for instance,
reprinted Wordsworth's "Goody Blake and Harry Gill" in
October 1799, along with "The Affectionate Heart" by
Joseph Cottle, "The Rose" by Sophia King, and "Morning"
by Charlotte King—the last two from a juvenile production
called *Trifles of Helicon* (1798). But the magazine reprintings do indicate a measure of acceptance. Both Byron and
Jeffrey, we remember, admitted in reviews of Wordsworth's later poetry that *Lyrical Ballads* was popular.[13]

Clearly Wordsworth was gaining some reputation as a
poet. An *Annual Review* article on Francis Wrangham's
Poems, a collection which is dated 1795 but apparently did
not come out until 1802, objects to the insertion of
undergraduate efforts of Wordsworth and Coleridge as

reprehensibly indelicate in view of the "high reputation which these gentlemen have deservedly attained." The same journal in 1803 literally shouted "STOP thief" at Peter Bayley for alleged plagiarism of Wordsworth in his *Poems*, particularly of "Tintern Abbey," from what the reviewer hails as "one of the finest passages that ever was or can be written."[14] Even the *Cabinet's* attack on *Poems in Two Volumes* (1807) takes its vehemence from the conviction, based on the "merit" of the *Lyrical Ballads*, that Wordsworth's was a "name of some celebrity" and he was "a man of genius" (April 1808). Amusing backhanded evidence of Wordsworth's reputation and influence for change is the fact that Anna Seward complained bitterly that "Mr. Hayley's once inventive, classical, and elegant muse, has of late appeared deplorably infected by Wordsworth's system concerning the propriety of using all sort of familiar terms in serious verse" (letter to Robert Fellowes; May 31, 1806).

The idea that the *Lyrical Ballads* was a failure, so confidently expressed by Christopher Wordsworth and Mrs. Oliphant, and so curious in the light of this evidence, probably derives largely from Joseph Cottle's negative statements in his *Early Recollections*: that the sale of the volume "was so slow, and the severity of most of the Reviews so great, that its progress to oblivion seemed ordained to be as rapid as it was certain," that he not only sold most of the first impression "at a loss," but when he went out of the publishing business in the fall of 1799 and disposed of his holdings to Longman's, the copyright of the *Lyrical Ballads* was judged to be worthless.[15] Why Cottle was in such a hurry to get rid of the *Lyrical Ballads* remains something of a mystery. Perhaps he did not value it very highly himself. Possibly, as Mrs. Moorman suggests (I, 441), he was put off by Southey, whose review in the *Critical Review*, we recall, was one of the most acrimonious, probably reflecting his personal relations with his brother-in-law Coleridge. Cottle's memory is certainly unreliable about the "severity" of most of the reviews, since the really vehement attacks on Wordsworth did not come until later; the central fact is probably that the publisher was anxious to pose as the unselfish recognizer and benefactor of genius, willing to bring out what nobody else then had the perception to appreciate. In fact, the *Lyrical Ballads* must be considered a qualified success which was bringing Wordsworth some notoriety.

The question is, what does this limited popularity mean? Does it indicate that Wordsworth was wrong in thinking his poems so different as not to be readily acceptable, or that he was gradually succeeding in creating—as he later said a poet must—the taste by which he was appreciated?[16] Probably some of both. Perhaps we can understand the situation better if we try to project ourselves backwards and see the *Lyrical Ballads* in the context of 1798— something difficult if not impossible to do, although our efforts in the third chapter to establish the critical environment may help.

For so long now we have thought of the work as a literary landmark, forgetting that many of the characteristics of that monument are the accumulation of age or the effects of perspective. The *Lyrical Ballads* of literary history is a composite document, made up of not only the small volume which Cottle published in 1798, but also the 1800 edition in two volumes, the 1800 Preface, with its additions, notably in 1802, and the aura cast around the whole by Wordsworth's other poetry, particularly *Poems in Two Volumes* of 1807, which seemed to some contemporaries to confirm or define the *Lyrical Ballads*.

If we continue trying to get back to 1798 and see the *Lyrical Ballads* against the contemporary background, we realize first that this was just another small book of miscellaneous poems, appearing anonymously from a provincial bookseller—one of many, with little to recommend

it especially to book-stall browsers of the day. It helps our
perspective to see in the *Anti-Jacobin Review and Magazine's* "Monthly List of Publications," under the heading
"Poetry. Novels," the announcement of the second issue—
"Lyrical Ballads, with a Few other Poems. 5/ Arch"—and
to note that the only other works of poetry listed by this
journal for that month (October 1798) were *Ode du Roi
de la Grande Bretagne* and *Poetical Trifles* by Elizabeth
Moody. This is in its way more enlightening than the
valuable summary of the literary activity of 1798 provided
by the *Annals of English Literature.* The editors list twenty-
eight authors of six volumes of verse, seven of plays, one
translation, five pieces of prose fiction, two biographical
works, one book of literary criticism, three travel books,
one study of education, two pieces of social criticism, and
three collected works. This listing certainly indicates an
active and various literary scene. Something of the range
is suggested by the distance between C.B. Brown's gothic
novel *Wieland*, Thomas Malthus's study of the *Principle
of Population*, and Thomas Morton's *Speed the Plough*
—now remembered for that precocious Victorian, Mrs.
Grundy. But the names, certainly of the poets, are
familiar ones: Coleridge, Cowper, Lamb and Lloyd,
Landor, Rogers, and, of course, Wordsworth. Here too is
indeed a range, from Landor's *Gebir* to Rogers' *Epistle to a
Friend*, suggesting something of the new effulgence and the
old restraint. The unknown Elizabeth Moody, however,
she of the *Poetical Trifles*, gives a more revealing insight
into the 1798 scene. Put beside that work Mary R. Stockdale's *The Effusions of the Heart: Poems* (1798), which was
"Dedicated, by Permission, to her Majesty," and which
according to the *Critical Review* affected a "querulous
tone." Add another important element in the setting of the
time: *The Sphinx's Head Broken; or a Poetical Epistle with
Notes, to Thomas James M*th**s . . . proving him to be the
Author of The Pursuits of Literature*, by Andrew Oedipus,
an Injured Author (1798), and we are beginning to get a

better picture of the thicket of publication in which the *Lyrical Ballads* experiment sprouted (see Appendix).

For a roughly contemporary view of the current poetical scene, we can turn to the ironical author of *The Campaign, to his Royal Highness, and Britannia in the Year One Thousand Eight Hundred* (1800). In *Britannia* he wrote:

> In vain the laurel'd wreath may Rogers hope,
> He flows too much like Goldsmith and Pope;
> And Cowper's frigid lay who can rehearse?
> He writes no blank, but cold Miltonic verse.
> Fastidious Bowles scorns all poetic art,
> Neglects the head, and only strikes the heart.
> Hark! Maurice sings in low and grating tones,
> The spurious virtues of seditious Jones;
> Vain was his science, vain his tuneful art,
> He liv'd and died a harden'd whig at heart.
> Man, equal man, licentious Woodhull sings,
> And spoils his lyre by democratic strings.
> Who but our Jacobins can Pye admire?
> His odes alone breathe no poetic fire.
> What dullness from unclassic Giffard flows,
> What beams of genius from Mathias' prose?
> His well wrought notes add music to his rhyme,
> As the pull'd rope give tinkling bells their chime;
> There, caustic, satire brilliant wit prevails,
> As bees bear stings, not in their heads but tails.
>
> (p. 44)

Another dyspeptic view, without names, was written in 1794 and published in 1799 by Alexander Thomson (*Pictures of Poetry; Historical, Biographical, and Critical*):

> For now the modern Muse can scarce produce,
> 'Mong all her toys, one earthly thing of use.
> At times she strikes the panegyric strings
> For vitious statesmen, or for worthless kings;
> Or, swell'd with Faction's vile malignant rage,
> Will Virtue's sons, and Freedom's friends engage.
> On elegiac strains she tries her art,
> Where neither Grief nor Nature claims a part;
> Or am'rous song, whose love is foreign to the heart,

With past'ral themes she now delights to play;
Weaves with dull care the flat insipid lay,
And many a couplet casts on sheep and goats away:
Or tiresome tales of mythologic lore,
To which, so often were they told before,
That sick Attention can attend no more.

                                                    (71-85)

It is noteworthy that David Rivers' two-volume *Literary Memoirs of Living Authors of Great Britain*, published in 1798, contains 1112 entries—including a write-up on Coleridge but not on Wordsworth. The *Gentleman's Magazine* reviewing it in May 1798 remarked, "The largest proportion treats on theological subjects; the next largest on poetical" (LXVIII, 414). This was, as Mayo has put it, an age of poetic inflation. The clergymen of the Established Church represented a fairly literate and fairly leisured class which naturally produced authors, of both sermons and verses. One of the most prolific was John Bidlake, B.A., Chaplain to his Royal Highness the Duke of Clarence, and Master of the Grammar School, Plymouth, author of *The Country Parson* (1797). Young ladies, like the Misses Moody and Stockdale, and their more famous sisters, Anna Seward and Mary Robinson, were also quite likely to publish a few effusions at the urging of friends, usually by subscription, some in handsome editions, wide-margined, hot-pressed, embellished with illustrations—as Anna Seward's *Original Sonnets on Various Subjects* (1799) sported a title-page engraving illustrating a passage from the first sonnet:

          Come, bright IMAGINATION come, relume
          Thy orient lamp!

Some in crude productions of provincial presses—as was Elizabeth Smith's *Life Review'd: A Poem; Founded on Reflections upon the Silent Inhabitants of the Church Yard*

of Truro, in the County of Cornwall (1782), which obviously anticipates the device of Wordsworth's *The Excursion*, and which has a long subscription list without the
usual display of titled names but rather identifying many
subscribers as tradesmen.

Even the first publisher of *Lyrical Ballads*, Joseph Cottle,
we remember, himself dabbled in verse and brought out in
1798 *Malvern Hills: A Poem*. Poets, indeed, sprang from
all walks of life. *Poetry Miscellaneous and Dramatic*
(Edinburgh, 1797) was signed "By An Artist." The stage
was represented by others than the fair Mary ("Perdita")
Robinson, including Thomas Hull of the Theater Royal,
Covent-Garden (*Moral Tales in Verse Founded on Real
Events* [1797]); George Colman, the Younger (*My Night-
Gown and Slippers; or Tales in Verse* [1797]); and George
Davies Harley, Comedian (*Holyhead Sonnets* [1800]). The
military also waxed poetical in all the ranks, from Captain
Thomas Morris and Lt. John Heyrick, Jr., to Corporal
Robert Brown and Private Soldier Steward Lewis. Within a
decade or so appeared the verse of James Heany, Bookbind-
er; Martin Archer Shee, R.A.; William Grant, Teacher of
Mathematics; Ann Yearsley, a Milkwoman of Clifton;
Thomas White, Master of the Mathematical School at
Dumfries; and Robert Bloomfield, a farmer's boy. David
Love, author of *A Few Remarks on the Present Times, with
a Serious Advice to the Redeeming of Time Here: so that
we may be blessed and happy when time shall be no more*
(1797?) describes himself simply as "a lame man, who
makes verses on any subject, if employed." The *Poetical
Register*, reviewing James Hogg's *The Mountain Bards*,
remarked: "The labouring class of society has, of late years,
teemed with poets and would-be poets. If it should much
longer display the same fertility, there will not be a single
trade or calling which will not have produced a bard."[17]

Something of the profusion of this poetic flow is suggested by the *Poetical Register and Repository of Fugitive*

Poetry for 1801, which provides a "Chronological List of Living Poetical Writers, according to the date of their earliest Poetical Publication," bearing the names of 113 men and fifteen women, including—as we saw in Chapter Three—"W. Wordsworth 1800." Through the preface of his *Poetical Prolusions* (1800), John Glanville apologized: "In this our day, a Volume of Poems is, perhaps, a Work of supererogation"—but obviously was not deterred. Oh, that saving "perhaps."

It is interesting to note also how early this poetic virus struck: Wordsworth at twenty-eight was relatively old for a poet. Of course he had published *An Evening Walk* when he was twenty-three, but even that was pretty far advanced in years. Thomas Dermody was not yet fourteen when his *Poems* (1789) came out, and William Dimond the Younger says that his *Petrarchal Sonnets and Miscellaneous Poems* (1800) are "the production of SIXTEEN." The author of *The Village Muse; or, A Poem of Summer* (1796) calls himself "Juvenis" and in an advertisement admits to eighteen. John Courtenay, Jr., whose *Juvenile Poems* were published in 1795, died a cadet engineer in Calcutta at the age of nineteen, and George Goodwin declares his *Rising Castle, with Other Poems* (1798) was written "at, and under the age of nineteen years."

The younger George Colman in his 1797 *My Night-Gown and Slippers; or Tales in Verse* has Tom, Dick, and Will discuss this mob of modern poets (p. 6):

> It cost them very little pains
> To count the modern Poets who have brains.
> 'Twas a small difficulty;—'twasn't any:
>   They were so few.
> But to cast up the scores of men
> Who wield a stump they call a pen,
> Lord! they had much to do!
>   They were so many.

William Gifford is still crueler about this poetic flood:

> This metromania, creeps thro' every breast;
> Now fools and children void their brains by loads,
> And itching grandams spawl lascivious odes;
> Now lords and dukes, curs'd with a sickly taste,
> While Burns' pure healthful nurture runs to waste,
> Lick up the spittle of the bed-rid muse,
> And riot on the sweepings of the stews.
> > (*Baviad* [London, 1800], p. 49)

Here speaks the crudity of a poet who himself had been a ship's boy and a cobbler's apprentice, and is currently the translator of Juvenal; but the quality of much of the contemporary verse is well enough summed up by Robert Farren Cheetham's *Odes and Miscellanies* (1796):

> Haste thee then, nymph, and live with me,
> I woo thee to my cot, sweet MEDIOCRITY!
> > (p. 53)

Indeed, most of these outpourings could hardly be ranked so high. The *Monthly Mirror* in reviewing J. Hucks' *Poems* (1798) remarked that it was no better than mediocre, "yet, such is the quality of verse with which the press is daily teeming, that even this is a station to which few writers are fortunate enough to arrive" (August 1798).

Many of these writers agreed in being quite modest about their poetical pretensions. Richard Cooksey charmingly prefaced his *Miscellaneous Poems* (1796) with the author's disclaimer: "*Poetry is not his Profession*; he rummages no old Trunks for Manuscripts of Shakespeare; disturbs not, by Criticism, the *Manes* of a *Wharton*; nor does he attempt to tear the Laurel from the Brows of *Pye*." To Edward Atkyns Bray, *Poems* (1799) were "the amusement of my leisure hours," and Mary Ann Chantrell called her *Poems on Various Subjects* (1798) "trifles," the work of an "inexperienced and unpolish'd muse." Richard Polwhele even labeled his 1796 volume *Poetic Trifles*, and Charlotte and Sophia King more elegantly entitled their productions *Trifles of Helicon* (1798). J.C. Cross's 1796 book (which had a subscription list including many theatrical people) was appropriately called *Parnassian Bagatelles: Being a Miscellaneous Collection of Poetical Attempts, &c.* As an epigraph for his *Poems on Several Occasions, including the Petitioner, or a View of the Red-Book* (1799), J.J. Vassar chose "Trifles light as Air," and in dedicating them to the "Friends of Idleness" declared "Genius denies them, Wit and Correctness both disclaim them, and Poetry disavows them." Mrs. Hale modestly said her *Poetical Attempts* (1800) were the "trifling productions of a female pen, chiefly written in the thoughtless years of youth, and never with a design of making them public." The anonymous "Lady" author of *Poems on Various Subjects* (1798) remarked in her dedication: "The following trifles were written with no intention of ever being presented to the view of my most partial friends, but merely to amuse a mind in constant danger of becoming a prey to serious and settled melancholy." At the beginning of his *Poems* (1799), the Rev. John Black offers a versified apology "for presuming to call these trifles, Poems," which concludes:

> All Affectation, I detest:—
> The title's short, and suits me best.

Although many of these protestations may be mock modesty, or attempts at warding off *hybris*, it is evident that at this time a great deal of light-weight, youthful, routine verse was being published. Much of it—as periodical critics often said bluntly—should never have seen print, and in other eras would not have. George Monck Berkeley —grandson of the Bishop—whose mother published his posthumous *Poems* in 1797 complete with an incredibly maternal 562-page life, made fun in his preface of the accepted reasons for publication: "he confessedly comes forward, neither urged by the entreaties of Friends, nor terrified by the threats of Creditors; and he certainly entertains no apprehension that his slender stock of Fame may be injured by the publication of spurious Copies, for none such exist." The last popular reason says something about the viability of verse in those days; as T. Morgan remarked in the preface of his *Poetry* (1797): "I first thought of putting my Poetry in Print when I found that many incorrect Copies had got abroad, and Pieces were attributed to me which I never saw." This in the town of Wakefield! And the reference to creditors' threats emphasizes that poetry was looked upon at the end of the eighteenth century as a plausible way to make money; it was, of course, mercenary motives that brought about the publication of *Lyrical Ballads*.

Volumes sold by subscription, as were a large number of those appearing at this time, were guaranteed some financial reward. Mrs. Hale's *Poetical Attempts* (1800), for example, which boasted four members of royalty, the Archbishops of Canterbury and York, and a long list of nobility among its subscribers, promised thereby to realize the authoress's laudable motive of "extricating an amiable and worthy family from their present difficulties." Some authors, like Wordsworth and Coleridge, were able to sell their verse to publishers, but many others printed their own, as Steward Lewis, Private Soldier in the Southern Fencibles, brought out in 1796 *Fair Helen of Kirkconnel, A Tragical Poem, Founded on Fact*, "Printed for the Author and sold in Behoof of his Family, Who are in Distress." In 1797 a French lady published a translation of Voltaire's *The Henriad* to recoup family losses.

Despite the routine character of much of this verse, and the modesty of many of the authors, we find some claims to originality and novelty, if not as sweeping as those of Wordsworth's "Advertisement," at least somewhat similar in purport. Clearly there was abroad the attitude De Quincey later expressed in the preface to his collected works: "to think reasonably upon any question, has never been allowed by me as a sufficient ground for writing upon it, unless I believed myself able to offer some considerable novelty."[18] Thomas Dermody pointed out in the Preface to his *Poems, Moral and Descriptive* (1800) that his main subjects had been touched upon but "never so diffusely handled, so that they may assert some claim to novelty." In comments which parallel Wordsworth's in his Preface the same year, Dermody confesses that:

an awful and enthusiastic veneration for the wild imagery, and fanciful flights of our ANCIENT BRITISH BARDS, may have enticed me too wide from that pointedness of temporary allusion, and those frothy ebullitions of eccentric whim, which so commonly disguise a vapid bottom, and which I perceive to be so highly prevalent over the mind of MODERN REFINEMENT.

He rejoices that his efforts at least "aspire to sense," which is more than can be said of "our late most celebrated authors, who rest their chief reputation on extravagant epithet, disgustful alliteration, and dazzling similarity of sound with sentiment" (pp. iii, v).

T. Morgan claimed that his *Pastoral Ballad*, although an imitation of Shenstone, was "as truly original as any thing that relates to Love can be" (*Poetry*, vi-vii). The Rev. John Sharpe said flatly that he presumed the subject of his *The Church, a Poem* (1797) was "novel and unprecedented." With considerable pomposity, Samuel Wilcocke plead for his *Britannia: A Poem* (1797):

The Author here deprecates the severity of criticism towards his present performance, in the first instance, with respect to the execution, in consideration of its being an early trial of skill in the Heliconian art; and, secondly, with respect to the novelty of the plan, and his deviation from common rules, in consideration that it is more arduous, as well as, if successful, more glorious, to climb the hill of poetic fame by a nearly unfrequented and rugged path, but which may, perhaps, be found to afford a firm and steady footing, than to follow the more commodious, but more slippery tracks which the numberless pilgrims, in all ages, towards the exalted fane on the mountain-top, have worn bare and broad, in continual progression. (pp. xii-xiii)

It is worth remembering also that in 1797 Coleridge thought Erasmus Darwin was "the first *literary* character in Europe, and the most original-minded Man." Not everyone approved the elaborate and elegant *Botanical Garden* (1789)—Coleridge said he "absolutely nauseate[d] it"[19]—and there was a good deal of Puritanical nose-lifting over the *Loves of the Plants,* and over Darwin's penchant, as *Pursuits of Literature* put it, to:

> Raise lust in pinks; and with unhallow'd fire
> Bid the soft virgin violet expire?
>   (6th ed., 1798; p. 18)

But Nathan Drake, defending modern poetry in his *Literary Hours* (1798), pointed out, "Dr. Darwin has lately favored the world with a poem perfectly original in its design";[20] and there was great interest in the novelty of the subject matter and treatment, the measured tripping of science in poetic dress. Botany became a popular study, even with young ladies, as represented decorously by *The Enchanted Plants, Fables in Verse* (1800) that Mrs. Montolieu wrote for her daughters—but went to unacceptable extremes according to some observers. Remarking, "How the study of the sexual system of plants can accord with female modesty, I am not able to comprehend," Richard Polwhele shuddered at the thought of the fair who:

> With bliss botanic as their bosoms heave,
> Still pluck forbidden fruit with mother Eve,
> For puberty in sighing florets pant,
> Or point the prostitution of a plant;
> Dissect its organ of unhallow'd lust,
> And fondly gaze the titillating dust.[21]

The fad also got attacked in 1798 along with another current rage in *The Lakers: A Comic Opera,* in which Veronica accepts a marriage proposal in this fashion: "Marry will I! We will be *connate* like the twin flowers on the same *peduncle*, and I will trust our love will be *sempervirent* and *perennial*" (p. 59).

Although John Sargent's *The Mine: A Dramatic Poem* (1785) has a melodramatic plot about a loyal wife who, disguising herself, shared her husband's captivity in prison mines, the author's real interest is obviously in gnomic machinery and a sort of Darwinian personification of fossils. Anna Seward effused "On Mr. Sargent's Dramatic Poem":

> With lyre Orphean, see a Bard explore
> The central caverns of the mornless Night,
> Where never muse perform'd harmonious rite
> Till now!
>
> (Sonnet XLVII 1-4)

Joseph Fawcett, writing under the pseudonym of Sir Simon Swan, Baronet, in "The Art of Poetry, according to the Latest Improvements" (*Poems*, 1798), makes fun of the mathematical novelties of Erasmus Darwin, and presents laurels to the poet who will:

> Soaring to heights no muse before e'er flew
> Paint the retentive vigour of the Screw!
>
> (p. 268)

Miss Seward has a sonnet "On the Use of New and Old Words in Poetry" in which she votes for novelty to the extent of judicious "liberal daring." The anonymous *Public Spirit: A Lyric Poem* (Dublin, 1797), probably by Peter Alley,[22] declares in an introductory "Observations on the Irregular Ode":

But, certainly, if innovation be dangerous, there is sometimes bigotry in habit; nor should even unpromising attempts be dismissed from the hastiness of scorn; since, to speak from experience, that which is now considered as useless or spurious, may derive recommendations from trial, and legitimation from time.

(p. 11)

Thus the *Lyrical Ballads* came out at a time that various kinds of poetic novelty were developed or claimed. This was an age that valued originality and tended to exaggerate it. The anonymous *Innovation: A Poem* (1799) declared, "Yes, bards can innovate," but was harshly critical of the results:

> From line to line the flickering splendors run,
> As varnish'd tea-boards glitter in the sun,
> See garish ornament, with painted face,
> No more content to hold the second place,
> In gay confusion human and divine,
> False, true, old, modern, present, past combine;
> O'er allegoric hyperbolic verse
> Trope after trope, an endless shower, disperse;
> Huge similies from page to page unroll,
> And form the texture of the flimsy whole
>
> (pp. 8-9)

The attitude toward poetic form expressed here is not very different from Wordsworth's, and helps explain why he spoke of his own innovation rather as restoration.

It appears, therefore, that the *Lyrical Ballads'* coming out as it did and when it did was commonplace: it was part of a flood of verse, often juvenile and confessedly trivial, against which Wordsworth's claims of novelty must be judged. Even those claims had an element of the commonplace about them, since innovation was in the air. But his claims were insistent and generally accepted, both in approval and in condemnation—with how much justice is a question for the next chapter.

CHAPTER SIX

The Originality
of the *Lyrical Ballads*

On September 29, 1798, at festivities and rural games held in Dorchester to celebrate the birthday of the Duchess of Wirtenberg, the contests included "A pound of tobacco to be grinned for," "A Michael-day goose to be dived for," and "Half-a-guinea for the best ass—in three heats" (*Annual Register*, p. 84). This event occurred about two weeks after the *Lyrical Ballads* were in Cottle's hands for publication, and a few copies had probably been issued—just after the Wordsworths and Coleridge were setting out for Germany. It is noteworthy that the tone of most of the poems in their little book was closer to that of the rural amusements than it was to that of most of the volumes of verse appearing about the same time. Wordsworth's contributions to the 1798 *Lyrical Ballads* were characteristically different from most prevailing poetry in being more realistic and down-to-earth, more vigorous and joyful, and less topical and faddish. Perhaps a survey of the poetry being published and read about 1798 will suggest something of the essential originality of the *Lyrical Ballads*.

In the preface to *Poems, Moral and Descriptive* (London 1800), Thomas Dermody made a significant comment on

current poetry, appropriately indicting it for its "pointedness of temporary allusion." Among the more than fifty
books of verse published in 1798 in the British Isles which
I have been able to see, many took some occasion to
comment on topical matters, and at least ten were predom-
inantly satires attacking some contemporary abuse.

As the *Monthly Mirror* remarked in July 1798, "Satire is
become of late so fashionable, that even character and
talent have no security from its shafts."[1] Of course this was
the heyday of *The Anti-Jacobin*, in which George Canning,
George Ellis, John Hookham Frere, and William Gifford
were lashing "the soft seductions, the refinements nice" of
the "new morality." But the continued popularity of the
eighteenth-century genre of satire covered a range of lesser-
known works from the light-hearted to the intense. In 1801
appeared *The School for Satire: or, A Collection of
Modern Satirical Poems written during the present reign*,
bearing the epigraph: "Satire is the Poetry of a Nation
highly polished."

Among the lighter satiric efforts of the period belong
Satires, &c. by Jaques (London, 1798), possibly *The Vision, A Poem Containing Reflections on Fasionable
Attachments, Fasionable Marriages, and Fashionable Education. By an Enemy to them all* [Thomas Grady] (Dublin,
1798), and certainly *The Sea-Side, a Poem, in Familiar
Epistles from Mr. Simkin Slenderwit, Summering at Ramsgate, to his Dear Mother in Town. The Second Edition,
with great Improvements, and an Appendix* (London,
1798). This amusing bit of fluffy doggerel devotes some
ninety pages to analysis of the mores of the beach set
and the practice of using bathing machines:

> Now tripping along come two maidens of blood;
> "O! give us a driver that's steady and good:
> "Who burns not at females quite naked to glance,
> "But can swin like a fish, if we meet a mischance.

"For Miss FIBER protests that whene'er we go in
" 'Tis by far the best way to strip quite to the skin."
(pp. 5—6)

The anonymous author of *The Patrons of Genius: A Satirical Poem. With anecdotes on their dependents, votaries, and toad-eaters, Part the First* (London, 1798), lays about him more vigorously, declaring in his preface: "No period of English History has so obviously and loudly required the chastisement of Satire as the present. All the vices of which Human Nature is susceptible, are sheltered under the masks of Religion, or Law, or Patriotism, or Loyalty:—a refined system of swindling prevades all the ranks and orders of society." He makes fun of the Poet Laureate thus:

Is there not PYE? Whene'er the sun sets out,
Pye makes an ode, and when he turns about;
And yet he hardly earns enough to dine.
One hundred pounds—one butt of Malmsey wine—

A long footnote concludes: "Pye would be *one-third a poet*; if he would *drink* his sack instead of *thinking* of it, or its giver; and if he would write from his own fancy, and forget his paltry Greek" (p. 5). The satirist is also arch about Wilberforce's efforts to enforce observations of the Sabbath:

Now Wilberforce his rampant cat restrains,
And separates his am'rous cocks and hens,
Lest, by hot blood impell'd, they seek a mate,
And on the Sabbath dare to copulate.
(pp. 38-9)

John Wolcot, or Peter Pindar as he called himself, was an exceedingly popular satirist of the day. His *Tales of the Hoy*, which was published in 1798 and went to four editions that year, attacks particularly contemporary journalism—in a tone that fits the 1970's.

Most of the satires appearing in 1798, however, were
related to the most notorious satirical production of the
time, Thomas James Mathias' anonymously published
The Pursuits of Literature, which came out in one part in
1794, by 1797 had grown to four parts revised, and went
on through sixteen editions by 1812. Its impact owed as
much to the long prose notes as to the uneven verse,
and most of all to the mystery of the authorship. This
mystery the pseudonymous Andrew Oedipus sought to
dispel in *The Sphinx's Head Broken: or, a Poetical Epistle*
(London, 1798):

> Long hast thou reign'd, fell demon of the night,
> Long aim'd at wit thy shaft, at worth thy spite;
> Long hiss'd malignant vapours in thy song,
> And play'd the dark assassin's game too long.
>
> (p. 5)

In much soberer vein is William Boscawen's anonymously
published *The Progress of Satire: An Essay in Verse, with
notes, containing remarks on "The Pursuits of Literature"*
(London, 1798), which declares in its preface, "Whether or
not it be for the interests of learning that almost every
writer should be assailed by the lash of anonymous satirists, and that the public should encourage, if not applaud
those satirists, may surely be a matter of serious doubt,"
and accuses *Pursuits of Literature* of:

> blending love of truth and zeal for right
> With bloated arrogance and envious spite.
>
> (259-60)

Signing his own name and rank, Thomas Dutton, A.M.,
takes 117 pages for his *The Literary Census: A Satirical
Poem; with Notes, &c. Including free and candid Strictures
on the Pursuits of Literature, and its anonymous Author*
(London, 1798), but like Mathias himself he has a very high
percentage of prose notes to verse. He remarks:

> Can I contend with Fashion's powerful sway,
> When SATIRE forms the *order of the day?*
>   (121-2)

and sneers at anonymity:

> Well may he dread to meet the public eye,
> For guilt appals, and bids the dastard fly.
>   (195-6)

Although Boscawen and Oedipus were critical of Mathias' spiteful attacks, both felt forced to express approval of his conservative stand on church and state. Richard Polwhele, however, in his own anonymous *The Unsex'd Females: A Poem Addressed to the Author of the Pursuits of Literature* (London, 1798), leans further over to the favorable side and accords the unknown author "a true poetical genius," since he can assert "on the best authority, that many in this country, whose politics and even religion have been long wavering, are now fixed in their principles" by this work. Polwhele is intent rather on making Mary Wollstonecraft his central villainess!

Of this whole prominent satiric strain in the poetry of the period, *Lyrical Ballads* shows scarcely an echo. Wordsworth had been interested in satire as recently as 1796-1797 and had worked on a modernization of Juvenal with his friend Francis Wrangham. But he lost his copy of Juvenal and nothing came of the project. Ten years later he wrote Wrangham that his contribution had been destroyed because he had "long since come to a fixed resolution to steer clear of personal satire" and was dubious about any kind.[2] Perhaps by the *Lyrical Ballads* he was already coming to the point of view he expressed in *The Prelude* that satire too easily partook:

> Of scorn and condemnation personal,
> That would profane the sanctity of verse.
>   (XI, 60-1)

The only clear evidence in *Lyrical Ballads* is from the earliest poem of the collection, "The Femal Vagrant," especially in the description of soldiers later cut from the *Guilt and Sorrow* version:

> the brood
> That lap (their very nourishment!) their brother's blood.
> (125-6)

Otherwise, topical allusions are almost lacking from *Lyrical Ballads*. The most conspicuous omission at this time is of references to the war with France. Besides the comments in "The Female Vagrant," the only mention of war is in the fact that the "Old Man Travelling" was going to see his mariner son who had been fatally wounded in a "sea fight." Perhaps Wordsworth's pro-French views were already changing by 1798 and he was less sure how he felt about the war. The same year as the *Lyrical Ballads*, however, Coleridge published "Fears in Solitude" and "France: An Ode," in which he recanted his own earlier support of France; and other poets publishing that year expressed a variety of attitudes toward the war. One of the most vigorous attacks is by Joseph Fawcett, in *Poems, to which are added Civilized War, Before published under the Title of the Art of War, With considerable Alterations* (London, 1798). "Civilized War" deplores

> the foul offence, th'enormous crime,
> Gigantic guilt of war.

This anti-war attitude finds a frequent voice, as in the title piece of H. Hughes' *Retribution, and Other Poems* (London, 1798):

> Can it be glory to destroy mankind;
>   To stamp destruction on each object fair;
> The free in slavery's galling chain to bind,
>   And with affliction's groans o'erload the air?

The pervasiveness of the theme in contemporary verse appears from its getting even into a topographical poem like the Rev. Luke Booker's *Malvern, a Descriptive and Historical Poem* (London, 1798):

> —May he who rules the earth make wars to cease
> In all the world! each hostile engine break;
>
> (pp. 57-8)

Or a collection of girlish verse like Charlotte and Sophia King's *Trifles of Helicon* (London, 1798). Charlotte writes of "War":

> See bloody Discord lift her envious head,
>   And shake the hissing serpents from her hair:
> Then o'er the earth see wild Confusion spread,
>   And hast'ning Evils beckon to despair.
>
> (p. 12)

In "The Maniac" the anonymous authoress of *Poems, By a Lady* (London, 1798) draws a picture of a distraught woman, something like a cross between Wordsworth's "Female Vagrant" and Martha Ray of "The Thorn," whose misfortunes clearly come from war, a monster luridly depicted:

> His eyes two fiery meteors blaze,
> And high his crested plumage plays—
> A murderous falchion arm'd his hand,
> The other grasp'd a flaming brand—
> Nature convuls'd, receives the fiend
> Whole oceans fly—rocks, mountains rend—
>
> (p. 5)

Curiously, George Goodwin (*Rising Castle, with Other Poems* [Lynn, 1798]) also has a poem called "The Maniac" in which the heroine goes mad when her husband dies on the battlefield. The hero of Charlotte Smith's "The Forest Boy" is likewise a victim of the "cold statesman" who "let loose the demon of war" (*Elegiac Sonnets, and Other Poems*, Vol. II [1797]).

J. Hucks, Fellow of Catherine Hall, Cambridge, who includes in his *Poems* (Cambridge, 1798) "Lines Addressed to S.T. Coleridge," calling him his earliest friend at the University, a man "aye big with schemes/ Air-built, of never-fading happiness" (p. 140), cries out in "The Retrospect": "O God of battles, when shall slaughter cease?" (p. 13) Another Cambridge Fellow, W. Smyth of St. Peters,[3] brought out in 1798 the second edition of his *English Lyrics* (Liverpool), containing an "Ode to Reason" written in 1794 in which he despaired of the irrationality of the warring age:

> Oh sweep from Memory's page,
> The records of our age!
> Lest every future sage, and chief of daring mind,
> To chill despair resign'd.
> Nor longer weave the great design,
> Nor toil with energy divine,
> But man for bliss unfit, nor for thy sway design'd,
> Impatient dream, and scorn his helpless kind.
>
> (p. 56)

Although Mary R. Stockdale's *The Effusions of the Heart: Poems* (London, 1798) is dedicated with permission to Her Majesty the Queen, it includes "The Remonstrance, An Ode on His Majesty's Birthday, June 4, 1797," which hails "much-lov'd" George but frankly regrets his involvement in the war.

Other contemporary reactions, however, were more patriotic. Robert Farren Cheetham, an undergraduate at Brasenose College, sent the King a copy of his 1798 *Poems* along with a letter hoping his Majesty would "design to bestow" upon him "one smile of complacence," and enclosing a manuscript blank verse poem of 107 lines "On the last splendid success of your Majesty's arms" which begins:

> Lives there a Man, whose cold and groveling soul
> Feels not the patriot glow of conscious pride,

When Glory, in her starry-lustred robe,
Deigns her immortal honours to bestow,
And, leaning from the skies, with angel-look,
Gilds with celestial beams the native isle?

The popular pose is reflected in a song performed at Covent
Garden for the first time on March 31, 1798, and published
in *Songs, Duets, Choruses &c, in the New Musical Piece
of the Raft; or Both Sides of the Water* (London, 1798).
Mr. Rivers sang:

Now proud vaunting Gaul, full of vapour and boast,
    Inflated, determines to give the world laws,
With heart and with hand to protect Britain's coast,
    We march on to conquer, or die in her cause;
Volunteer it to glory with true patriot fire,
And this is the watch-word our corps shall inspire,
    "Britons strike home, revenge your country's wrongs."

(p. 3)

More jingoistic is Thomas Maurice, an assistant keeper of
the British Museum and popularizer of Indian antiquities,
in *The Crisis of the British Muse to the British Minister
and Nation* (London, 1798). He calls upon his countrymen
to:

With tides of Gallic blood expunge their stains,
And shew mankind that God TH'AVENGER, reigns,

and asks in hawkish contempt:

But, are there dastards so deprav'd and base
To pant for PEACE with this detested race?

(pp. 17, 22)

Similar in tone are Percival Stockdale's *The Invincible
Island; A Poem; with Introductory Observations on the
Present War*, which appeared in 1797, and the anonymous
*Delenda est Carthago; or, a Poetical Paraphrase on the
French Declaration*, published at Margate in 1798. The
latter begins:

> Ye glorious sons of renovated Gaul,
> Who set up mobs, and bid their rulers fall,
> Who—train'd to rapine, and inur'd to blood,—
> Have pour'd o'er Europe your devouring flood.

Thus in a variety of modes, and covering the attitude spectrum from dove to hawk, the war with France was in 1798 a much more popular poetic subject than the *Lyrical Ballads* would reveal. Indeed, the pressing interest in the war at the time suggests that Wordsworth's 1798 poems were almost escapist in largely ignoring the whole contemporary scene—and thus notably different from his earlier *Descriptive Sketches*.

Aside from the war background of "The Female Vagrant," there is no significant allusion to contemporary events in the *Lyrical Ballads*; and except for the reference to Collins' "Ode on the Death of Thomson" in "Lines Written Near Richmond," no mention of any recognizable individuals—and even that depends on a footnote. Wordsworth's was certainly not the only collection of verse published in 1798 to ignore the larger current scene in favor of more personal, fanciful, or allegorical subjects. The writer of *Poems on Various Subjects*, By a Lady (London, 1798), for instance, offers such verses as "To Adversity," "To Fancy," and "Written by the Desire of a Gentleman to his Mistress." Nevertheless, it is noteworthy that after Edmund Burke died in 1797, Mrs. West published *An Elegy on the Death of the Right Honourable Edmund Burke* (London, 1797) and the Rev. John Chetwood Eustace turned out *An Elegy to the Memory of the Right Honourable Edmund Burke* (London 1798); while Wordsworth, who heard Burke in London and later included an appreciative passage about him in *The Prelude*, did not put this kind of poem in the *Lyrical Ballads*.

By contrast, C.A. Esq. tuned his *Britain's Genius; A Song* (Bath, 1797) to condemn the recent mutiny in the Royal

fleet at The Nore. Robert Cheetham (*Poems* [Stockport,
1798]) wrote verses "On the Frustrated Attempt of the
French to Invade Ireland"; Mary Ann Chantrell, of Newington Butts, printed in *Poems on Various Subjects* (London, 1798) lines on the health of the King of England and
the death of the King and Queen of France; H.F. Cary
published in 1797 *Ode to General Kosciusko*; John Gisborne even brings an attack on Catherine the Great and
praise of George Washington into *The Vales of Wever,
a Loco-Descriptive Poem* (London, 1797) and the same
year published *Elegy to the Memory of the Rev. William
Mason*, who had just died. In his *Poems on Several
Occasions, Written Chiefly in the remoter Parts of Cumberland and Northumberland* (London, 1797), John Jackson includes "Burning of Tom Paine in Effigy" and "To
a Very Young Lady, Upon her quitting the room in some
confusion, after striving in vain to repress her tears,
while the author was reading, to a circle of friends,
the will of the late unfortunate Louis XVI"—a title which
will vie with Wordsworth's most prolix. In the same vein
are *Public Spirit: A Lyric Poem; occasioned by the Exemplary Zeal, Resolution and Decorum, Uniformly manifested by the Yeomanry Corps of Ireland, in the Sacred
Cause of their King and Country* (Dublin, 1797); *The
Battle of the Nile, a Poem* (London, 1799) by William
Sotheby; and Mrs. Jane West's "To the Island of Sicily:
Written after the Retreat of the King and Queen of Naples,
Dec. 1798" (*Poems and Plays* [London, 1799]). An amusing
example of poetic exploitation of the topical is *Capell's
Ghost, to Edmund Malone, Esq., Editor of Shakespeare*
(1799), which pictures Malone celebrating the recent ex-
posure of the forger Ireland when the ghost of Edward
Capell, an earlier editor, rises with 300 clerks and demands
vengeance for his ruin.

When George Berkeley saw a production of Greathead's
The Regent, he wrote "Verses on Seeing the Tragedy of the

Regent. To Bertie Greathead, Esq." (*Poems*, 1797). Eliza
Daye also put into verse her "Thoughts Occurring in the
Theater, on Seeing Mrs. Siddons in the Character of
Belvidera" (*Poems on Various Subjects* [1798]). According
to Hazlitt's report, Wordsworth in early 1798 saw Monk
Lewis' *Castle Spectre* and thought "it fitted the taste of the
audience like a glove" (Howe, XVII, 118). Some of these
feelings show in the 1800 Preface, but not in the verse of
Lyrical Ballads.

One of the most striking omissions from the currently
popular subjects in *Lyrical Ballads* is any reference to
slavery and the slave-trade. In 1798 William Wilberforce's
annual motion for the abolition of the slave-trade, a cause
in which he had been agitating since 1789, almost carried—
83 yes to 87 no. With the help of Thomas Clarkson,
who had a farm at Ullswater and came into the Wordsworth orbit in 1800 when Dorothy wrote her friend Jane
Marshall about this man "who took so much pains about
the slave trade" (*EY*, p. 300), Wilberforce finally succeeded
in passing the motion in 1807. Although as late as 1804 a
pamphlet was published entitled "A Defence of the Slave
Trade on the grounds of humanity, policy and justice,"
the conscience of Britons was aroused at their mercenary
role in this enterprise. The Rev. William Bagshaw Stevens
comments in his journal on August 20, 1797, about his
experiences in Liverpool: "Viewed a Guinea ship capable of
holding 450 Negroes. Slaves at prime cost 7 sold again for
70. This Boat last year cleared for her owners 7000.
Throughout this large-built Town, every Brick is cemented
to its fellow Brick by the blood and sweat of Negroes."[4] As
usual, poets—ranging from Cowper to Perdita Robinson to
John Wolcot—reflected and pricked the conscience of the
nation, and their utterance took many forms. Captain
Thomas Morris published in 1796 *Quashy, or the Coal-
Black Maid. A Tale*, which bitterly curses the supporter of
slavery:

> May each woo'd virgin loathe the wretch's bed;
> With beasts, in deserts, may the monster dwell;
> And furies haunt him from the depths of hell.
>
> (44-6)

Even Ann Yearsley, the Milkwoman of Bristol, brought out *A Poem on the Inhumanity of the Slave-Trade* (London, 1788), declaring elegantly, "Custom, thou hast undone us!" In 1798 anti-slavery was one of the subjects of Mary Stockdale's *The Effusions of the Heart*, and John Jamieson's *Eternity, a Poem: Addressed to Freethinkers and Philosophical Christians* described "dark Afric's son" invoking the immortality which will free him from the oppression of "free-born Britons." Most startling, the Rev. Benjamin Johnson (*Original Poems*) warned his countrymen:

> Blush Britons!—blush! perhaps a day may come,
> When ruthless hands may force you from your home;
> To *Afric's* shores again may *Commerce* roll,
> And sable plund'rers riot in your spoil;
>
> (pp. 33-4)

This slavery theme was also handled variously by Edward Bray (*Poems*, 1799), H.F. Cary, *Ode to General Kosciusko*, 1797, William Dimond the Younger, *Petrarchal Sonnets, and Miscellaneous Poems*, 1800, and Mrs. Hale, *Poetical Attempts*, 1800. In 1797 John Gorton's *Tubal to Seba. The Negro Suicide*, a bad poem with portentous epic echoes, saw a second edition embellished with a sensational engraving of a black about to plunge a knife into his bosom.

Wordsworth's explanation in *The Prelude* for his not being interested in this popular subject, which he found in contention around him when he returned to England from France, was his confidence

> That, if France prosper'd, good Men would not long
> Pay fruitless worship to humanity,

And this most rotten branch of human shame,
Object, as seem'd, of a superfluous pains
Would fall together with its parent tree.
                    (1805, X, 223-7)

Clarkson apparently shared this belief and even went to
France to try to implement it there, but by 1798 he was
attacking the problem in England, as Wordsworth might
have also if the *Lyrical Ballads* had operated at that level.

Later Wordsworth did write poems about contemporary
men and events, for example: "To Touissant l'Ouverture,"
"Brave Schill! by death delivered, take thy flight," "The
French Army in Russia, 1812-13." He even wrote a not-
very-good sonnet to Clarkson in 1807 when the Abolition
of the Slave Trade act was finally passed: "Clarkson! it was
an obstinate hill to climb." But this was all after the great
"experiment" was over, and when Wordsworth was consciously producing more conventional poetry. There is
nothing in the first edition to match the contemporary
*A Congratulatory Poem on the Escape of Sir Sidney
Smith from France and his Happy Arrival in England.* The
events of the *Lyrical Ballads* were the small happenings of
daily life—hewing out an old stump, selling a lamb,
watching an old man go slowly by. The characters were not
people whose names were recognizable on the national
scene—contrast R. Anderson's sonnet "To John Horne
Tooke, Esq." hailing him as "Champion of freedom, friend
to all mankind" (*Poems on Various Subjects* [Carlisle,
1798], p. 122). Wordsworth did not "entirely approve" of
Tooke's character anyway (letter to Matthews, December
24, 1794, *EY*, 137), but another radical activist, John
Thelwall, had visited at Alfoxden in 1797 without being
mentioned in verse. The people Wordsworth was celebrating now were the unknown and the unsung, humble,
simple folk whose lives were circumscribed by narrow
limits and who, like the family in "The Brothers," were not

even recorded on grave stones, but survived only in local memory. Their importance was not in who they were or what they did, but what they felt.

Although the pieces in *Lyrical Ballads* often show obvious affinities with current verse in their narrative qualities, it is noteworthy that Wordsworth avoids the popular designation "tale." Only one poem in the collection is so titled, and that is Coleridge's "The Foster-Mother's Tale," a fragment from his tragedy *Osorio.* As close as Wordsworth comes is to give "Goody Blake and Harry Gill" the subtitle, "A True Story."

Although Romaine Joseph Thorn did not attach a generic subtitle to his popular *The Poor Boy* (1799), he pointed out in prefatory remarks, "The following little Tale was written nearly two years ago, and not withstanding the simplicity of its language, has been more cordially received by the public [it had been published in periodicals] than I could have expected." Poems labeled "tales" were, indeed, common to the point of becoming a fad around the time of the *Lyrical Ballads.* They included such variety as Bray's "Conrad and Phoebe. A Fairy Tale"; Dimond's "Lorenzo and Rosella; A Tale, in Stanzas"; West's "Henry, The Maniac, a Tale," "Fingal in Lochlin: A Tale," and "Alleyne and Ella, A Legendary Tale"; and from an anonymous "Artist", "The dutiful Wife. A Lyric Tale"—neatly balanced by "The Prostitute, A Lyric Tale." There is also John Black's "A Traditionary Tale," George Cumberland's *Lewina the Maid of Snowdon, A Tale,* Donoughue's "Hamet and Almena, an Oriental Tale," Robinson's "The Confessor. A Sanctified Tale," Whalley's *Edwy and Edilda: A Tale, In Five Parts,* Whitehead's *Atys and Adrastus, A Tale in the Manner of Dryden's Fables,* Helen Maria William's "An American Tale," and Yearsley's "Lucy, A Tale for the Ladies." George Colman the Younger published *Tales in Verse,* Robinson *Lyrical Tales,* and Hull

Moral Tales in Verse, Founded on Real Events. George Davies Harley's *Ballad Stories, Sonnets, &c* included "Egbert and Ellen. A Tale." This boy-girl title was especially popular, often with medieval, Nordic or oriental names, as in E.S.J.'s *Hildibrand & Una; or, The Knight and the Horse that never wearied* and, in *Poems* "Edwin and Eltrude. A Tale" and "Hoder and Heda. A Tale"; Englesfield Smith's "Sir Mordac and Balma. A Tale"; Elizabeth Hands' "Leander and Belinda. A Tale," and even Alexander Wilson's delightful Scottish piece, "Watty and Meg, or the Wife Reformed. A Tale." Bray included among his "Ballads" five poems with such paired titles as if this were recognized as the standard ballad form—although in fact it was not a characteristic pattern among the ancient ballads.

The volumes of verse which saw the light the same year as *Lyrical Ballads* included among them "The Monk of La Trappe: A Tale (Hannah Brand, *Plays and Poems* [Norwich, 1798]), "The Happy Villagers, A Tale" (Mary Ann Chantrell, *Poems on Various Subjects*), "Edgar and Emma. A Tale" (H. Hughes, *Retribution, and Other Poems*), simply "A Tale" (John Hunter, *A Tribute to the Manes of Unfortunate Poets*), "Doncaster Butter-Cross, A Whimsical Tale," which was a rather naughty story by the Rev. Benjamin Johnson (*Original Poems*), "Arthur and Ellen, A Tale" (*Poems on Various Subjects. By a Lady*), "Henry and Mary. A Tale" (Mary Stockdale, *The Effusions of the Heart*), and Peter Pindar's *Tales of The Hoy*, which in fact contained few tales, but professed to be a frame-sequence in the vein of Boccaccio and Chaucer. It does include "The Widow of Ephesus; A Tale"—the story of a weeping widow who promptly digs up her husband's body and substitutes it on a gibbet to save a new swain.

In such a setting, Wordsworth's failure to call his narratives "tales" must have some significance; it probably indicates his disinclination to associate himself with a

popular and often facile and shallow form. With some
justice he tells the reader toward the end of "Simon Lee":

> And I'm afraid that you expect
> Some tale will be related.

Such was indeed the general expectation of much contemporary verse, and Wordsworth is clearly announcing
a difference:

> It is no tale; but should you think,
> Perhaps a tale you'll make it.

His narratives required a good deal more "thinking" than
was characteristic of the stories so common to the magazines and collections of poetry.

Not only does Wordsworth in *Lyrical Ballads* refuse to
use the common generic tag of "tale," but he is exceedingly
and uncommonly chary of any genre designations in the
1798 edition. The only other poems of his to be put in
classes are "Old Man Travelling," which has the subtitle
"Animal Tranquility and Decay, A Sketch" (to become
the title in 1800), and "The Complaint of a Forsaken
Indian Woman." Contemporary collections of verse, on
the other hand, seem typically genre conscious. They
sometimes are organized by genre, frequently designate
genres, and often run the gamut indicated by the full
title of John Wolcot's *Pindariana; or Peter's Portfolio.
Containing Tale, Fable, Translation, Ode, Elegy, Epigram,
Song, Pastoral, Letters. With Extracts from Tragedy,
Comedy, Opera &c.* (London, 1794). And Peter left out
some favorites, such as the epitaph, the inscription, (of
which Wordsworth's "Lines left upon a Seat in a Yew-tree"
may be considered a variant), and above all, the sonnet.

It is certainly noteworthy that the *Lyrical Ballads* includes no sonnets, although the "other poems" of the title
at least would allow for them, as it did, for instance,
in George Goodwin's *Rising Castle, with Other Poems*

(1798). Wordsworth had toyed with the sonnet, perhaps as early as 1786, and preserves an example in his collected works to which he gives the title "Written in Very Early Youth." His first published poem was in this genre, "Sonnet on Seeing Miss Helen Maria Williams Weep at a Tale of Distress," which appeared in *The European Magazine* in March 1787 over the signature "Axiologus." This poem, however, Wordsworth never reprinted, and seems to have dismissed from his memory, with most of his early son-neteering, since he told Miss Fenwick that he "took fire" from Dorothy's reading to him some of Milton's sonnets in 1801 and wrote the first sonnets of his career "except an irregular one at school."[5] This school poem, Reed conjectures plausibly, is probably yet another one, also written in 1787, "Sonnet Written by Mr.—Immediately after the Death of His Wife."[6] Although Wordsworth later wrote over 500 sonnets—including some superb poems— and valued those of Shakespeare, Donne, and Milton, he obviously remained defensive enough about the genre to feel it necessary to write his famous "Scorn not the sonnet." He even declared to Landor, on April 20, 1822, that he used to think the genre "egregiously absurd," and if he had not fallen into the practice of composing sonnets, he "might easily have been better employed" (*LY*, I, 71).

The fact is, that the *Lyrical Ballads* appeared at a time when sonnets, to a mistress's eyebrow or less, were exceed-ingly popular. The Rev. John Black (*Poems* [Ipswich, 1799]) even indited one "On the Untimely fate of a fly, which lost its life in the Eye of a beautiful Lady." In the preface to *The Grove*, probably published in 1798, T.J. Mathias quoted *The British Critic*: "we confess ourselves tired to death with sonnets." But versifiers and the reading public apparently were not. William Lisle Bowles' wan *Fourteen Sonnets, Elegiac and Descriptive*, which came out in 1789—when Wordsworth was so struck with them that he kept his brother waiting while he sat in a niche of

London Bridge to finish reading them—by 1800 had gone
through seven editions. Charlotte Smith's *Elegiac Sonnets
and other Poems*, published first in 1784, continued to
grow and by 1811 had seen ten editions in the British
Isles. In 1799 two printings of *Original Sonnets on Various
Subjects* by Anna Seward, the Swan of Lichfield, were
called for, and Miss Seward flattered herself that her
ninety-one sonnets had vanquished the notion that the
English language was "not capable of doing justice to the
regular sonnet."

Most of the collections of verse published in 1798
included poems called sonnets, and most of them belonged
to that genre; although the name "sonnet" at the end
of the eighteenth century had not yet become finally
fastened to a specific form, but might be applied to any
little song, so that some of the poems labeled "sonnets"
were in a variety of shapes. Charlotte and Sophia King
call many of their verses sonnets, even though none is
even fourteen lines in length. Most are in quatrains of
varying numbers, up to seven, and one of Sophia's "sonnets" entitled "Love," is as brief as this:

> Tripping across the mead,
>   To cull the sweets of spring,
> An angry insect from the painted flowers
>   Darted its sting:
> So Love, in ambush, to beguile the hours,
>   Sent forth his feather'd dart
>   To wound my heart;
> Then, laughing, fled.
>
>   (p. 2)

In the same way Eliza Daye (*Poems, on Various Subjects*
[Liverpool, 1798]) obviously uses "song" and "sonnet"
interchangeably, and the thirteen poems given the latter
rubric exhibit different forms, frequently quatrains mixing
tetrameter and trimeter verse. Hence the Swan prided
herself on her "regular" or "legitimate" sonnets. A more

standard production of the time is "To a Summer Evening."
from M. Holford's *Gresford Vale, and Other Poems* (London, 1798):

> Now the day's last purple gilds the evening scene,
>   Now sounds the shepherd's pipe along the glade,
> Mild zephyrs whisper 'mong the willows green,
>   Whose leafy branches cast a browner shade.
> Now with light heart the peasant homeward hies,
>   With carols blithe he hails the departing day;
> The wild rose dipp'd in Nature's purest dies,
>   With odours sweet rewards the rustic lay.
> Ah! who can contemplate the peaceful cot,
>   Or sit beneath yon mountain's fringed brow,
> And view the village swain's contented lot,
>   Envying the joys which pomp and greatness know!
> Far from the precincts of the proud and vain
> In yon green wood I'll tune the past'ral strain.
>
> (p. 15)

It was no doubt this kind of thing which Wordsworth
thought absurd, and his own "On Seeing Miss Helen
Maria Williams Weep at a Tale of Distress" was egregious
enough. It began:

> She wept.—Life's purple tide began to flow
> In languid streams through every thrilling vein
>
> (*PW*, I, 269)

Leaving sonnets out of *Lyrical Ballads* was in rebellion
against this popular sniveling, and one declaration of the
volume's difference. It was also partly a repudiation of
Wordsworth's own early imitative style, just as his not
using the heroic couplet was a revulsion from the manner-
isms of his *An Evening Walk* and *Descriptive Sketches* as
well as a departure from current practices. For well over
half of the volumes of verse published in 1798 which I
have seen included some poems written in heroic couplet,
and about 40 per cent were exclusively in that meter. It
seemed to be the accepted versification for satire, and was

used also for a variety of other genres. The delayed posthumous *Poems* (Doncaster, 1802) of Mrs. Charles (Eliza Kirkham Strong) Matthews even contained poems called "odes" written in heroic couplet.

About two-thirds of the collections of verse published in 1798 which I have been able to look at contain one or more poems under the label "ode." The popularity and variety of this genre in the period can be indicated by the range from the *Ode on the Fluctuations of Civil Society* (London, 1797), in which strophe, antistrophe, and epode are elaborately marked, to J. Guy's *Songs, Consisting of Political, Convivial, Sentimental, Pastoral, Satirical, and Masonic* (London, 1797), which felt it necessary—despite the title—to include "An Ode to Winter:"

> Now bleakly blows the winter's wind,
>   And nipping frost the blood doth chill
> Now sick'ning nature lays reclin'd,
>   Nor can, as us'd, our wants fulfill.
>   (p. 88)

Evidently Wordsworth deliberately omitted odes from *Lyrical Ballads* as part of his attempt to present something more fundamentally simple than the run-of-the-mine collection of poetry. In the Preface to his 1815 *Poems* he notes that "the Lyrical" contains "the Hymn, the Ode, the Elegy, the Song, and the Ballad" (*Prose Wks.*, III, 27), but for the *Lyrical Ballads*, even including the few "other poems," he did not want to claim or suggest the higher and more elaborate reaches of the lyric note. This is clear from his comment in a note in the 1800 edition of that work, in which he observes that he "had not ventured to call" his "Tintern Abbey" an ode, although "it was written with a hope that in the transitions, and the impassioned music of the versification, would be found the principal requisites of that species of composition" (*PW*, II, 517).

Except for the satires, which were often vigorous
enough, most of the poetry published around 1798 was
elegiac and sentimental in tone. Mary Stockdale addressed
the reader at the beginning of her *The Effusions of the
Heart: Poems* (London, 1798): "Art thou the Child of
Misfortune? has Sorrow been the inmate of thy bosom?
has the sympathetic heart ever learned to sign over the
troubles of a beloved friend? or dost thou yet weep
over one who, shrouded for ever in the cold, the silent
tomb, has now paid the debt, the awful, certain debt
of mortality?/ If sorrows, such as these, have afflicted thy
tender breast, this little Volume is written for thee"
(pp. 10-11).

Surely some of the prevalent melancholy seeped into the
Lyrical Ballads. The "O woe is me! oh misery!" on which
"The Thorn" ends sounds a note echoed by the despair
of "The Female Vagrant":

> She wept;—because she had no more to say
> Of that perpetual weight which on her spirit lay.
>
> (269-70)

"Simon Lee," "The Last of the Flock" and "The Complaint
of a Forsaken Indian Woman" all have strains of sadness
in them. In Volume Two the pattern is continued with
"The Brothers," "Hart-leap Well," "Lucy Gray," "Ruth,"
"The Childless Father" and "Michael." It is understandable
that the *Monthly Mirror* should regret that the 1800
Lyrical Ballads was "marked by a querulous monotony of
woe, which we cannot applaud" (XI, 389). It is interesting,
however, that Wordsworth called none of his poems
elegies, and the whole atmosphere of the 1798 volume
contrasts markedly with such a collection as Robert Lovell
and Robery Southey's *Poems: Containing The Retrospect,
Odes, Elegies, Sonnets, &c.* (Bath, 1795), which deals
largely with historical, allegorical, and mythological subjects, and includes poems on "The Faded Flower" (Southey)

and "To Sensibility" (Lovell), and lines like these from Southey's "To Lycon":

> And does my friend again demand the strain,
>   Still seek to list the sorrow-soothing lay?
> Still would he hear the woe-worn heart complain,
>   When melancholy loads the lingering day?
>
> (p. 86)

This is the kind of poetry the essence of which John Hackett tries to isolate in the preface to his *Poems, Elegiac and Miscellaneous* (London, 1804): "unless the conceptions affect, by their tenderness, the finer cords of the heart, and arouse its dormant and susceptible feelings, presumptuous as I may be deemed, I boldly venture to assert, that there exists no merited claim to the nobleness of the appelation" (p. vii). Such muted, feminine quality of "tenderness" was characteristic of the poetry of Cowper and Bowles, as well as of the many lady poetasters of the day. The tone is strongly marked in Charles Lloyd and Charles Lamb's *Blank Verse* (London, 1798), of which the *Analytical Review* (May 1798) declared: "The whining monotonous melancholy of these pages is to us extremely tiresome." The *Monthly Mirror*, however, more attuned to the mode, found the pauses sufficiently varied "to prevent satiety" and praised "good sense, sound philosophy, and genuine piety" (August 1798).

By comparison with most contemporary verse, then, Wordsworth's style was more masculine, more vigorous, more down-to-earth. His poems partake at least as much of the head as of the heart, and are touched with common sense, lightened with humor, and warmed by a pervasive note of joy. For despite the "misery" of forsaken women and the clear-eyed awareness of the woes of mankind, *Lyrical Ballads* insists on the joy of life. Coleridge's "The Nightingale" is a denial of literary melancholia, and its positive protest: "In nature there is nothing melancholy"

(15) is almost a leitmotif of the whole collection. Even the recluse of "Lines left upon a seat in a Yew-tree" sighs with "mournful joy" (39); Martha Ray of "The Thorn" was once "blithe and gay" (119); and the "Female Vagrant" began a life of "thoughtless joy" (6), was loved by her husband "in joy" and looked upon the sea "Until it seemed to bring a joy to my despair"(144). Goody Blake delights in winter winds that bring down rotten boughs—"Oh joy for her" (49), "The Idiot Boy's" lips burr "with joy" (19) and he is "idle all for very joy" (86). How "blithe the throstle sings" (13) in "The Tables Turned," preaching nature's gospel of joy, just as on the first mild day of March:

> There is a blessing in the air,
> Which seems a sense of joy to yield
> ("Lines . . . sent by my little Boy", 5-6)

"The Convict" begins on a note of "the joy that precedes the calm season of rest" (3) and "The Mad Mother" ends in a maniac "now laugh and be gay" (99). The energy of "Hart-Leap Well" (first poem in the second volume) derives from the counterpoint of pleasure and pain developing from the opening:

> Joy sparkled in the prancing Courser's eyes;
> The horse and horseman are a happy pair;
> (9-10)

This constant awareness of the pervasive vitality of joy gives Wordsworth's recognition of the sorrows of things another dimension—a vivid quality at once taut, sensuous, ironic—which divides most of his lines from the muted, decorous, delicate melancholy of so much contemporary verse.

The hard-headedness of Wordsworth's tone in the *Lyrical Ballads* separates him also from the current crop of versifiers who delighted to sentimentalize the life of the

country and the poor. True, Crabbe had already etched
"the real Picture of the Poor" (*The Village*, 5), and the
Rev. Benjamin Johnson seemed to be carrying on the
naturalistic realism in such verses as "A Descriptive Poem"
(*Original Poems*, 1798):

> How dreary, dismal, desolate the scene!
> The land how barren!—cottages how mean!
>
> (p. 54)

Two years later John Bidlake, in his *The Summer's Eve.
A Poem*, objects to "poet's fancy-dreams of the rural
bow'r":

> See yonder hovel! mark the tottering roof!
> Against no angry pelting tempest proof:
>
> (p. 38)

Injustices to the poor are the theme of Samuel Pratt's
popular *Cottage-Pictures; or, The Poor: A Poem* (1801).
But Johnson also writes in "The Husbandman":

> Ambition breaks not his repose,
>   Nor robs his soul of rest;
> For envy, hate, corroding care,
> The dire effects of fell despair,
>   Are strangers to his breast.

This is the vein of romanticizing the lot of the peasants
which is common around the turn of the century. George
Monck Berkeley (*Poems* [1797]) paints this rosy picture
in "Evening, A Pastoral":

> Dews descending bless the soil,
> Eve suspends the peasant's toil;
> O'er the pansy-chequer'd plains
> Whistling tread the jocund swains;
>
> (p. 21)

So the jocund swains, innocent of envy, hate, and care, trip
happily through much "pastoral" poetry of the time.

J.C. Cross (*Parnassian Bagatelles* [1796]) practically drools in "The Happy Cottager, A Pastoral Ballad":

> Away from the town, from its tumult and strife,
>   Serenely to dwell be my lot;
> And in rural content, all the days of my life,
>   Let me happily pass in yon Cot!

In *The Hop-Garden, A Didactic Poem* (1799)—a run-over from his *Malvern* (1798), Luke Booker described how the poor retire:

> To rest; and lodg'd in hovels and in barns,
> Far sweeter sleep than oriental kings
> Encanopied by purple starr'd with gold.
>   (515-17)

Sometimes Booker's sentimental glow has a religious basis, as do the *Petrarchal Sonnets and Miscellaneous Poems* (1800) of William Dimond the Younger. Dimond's sonnet "On a Wandering Beggar-Boy" recognizes "what ills thou must endure," but comforts:

> Yet cheer thee, wretch! for *this* world's miseries o'er,
> *Another*, and a *better* one, remains in store.
>   (p. 46)

Wordsworth valued Crabbe's work, but questioned the accuracy of some of his sketches, which he thought verged on "the meanest kind of satire" and showed a "misanthropic vein."[7] His own view had less acid in it, without being pollyannishly sentimental either. He supplies the *"flow* of *feeling"* he found lacking in Crabbe, but he does not romanticize his characters. His people are simple, enduring folk who know joy and sorrow. Simon Lee is pathetic, but he once was merry and famous—known for at least four counties round. Although he is poor and weak, he still rejoices at the call of the hounds. His tragedy is the common human one that he has lived too long: he has outlived not only his usefulness but also his natural protectors—he is "the sole survivor." There is no suggestion that he has been exploited and cast aside: not only is his master dead, but no successor lives in the hall of Ivor. He has his little plot of ground; he is just too feeble to tend it properly. It is sad that he should be so helpless, that his weak ankles swell and he is forced to be so grateful for so little aid. The bite is in that irony, the disproportionate gratitude which emphasizes how little the young can really do for the old. The poem is on the familiar *sic transit* theme, but in how uncouth and novel a form. With deliberate roughness and hominess, and an awkward garrulity of persona which puts off many readers, Wordsworth domesticates the motif. He does it with feeling, but in a vivid, tough way which has nothing of the sentimental in it. The cliché imagery ("His cheek is like a cherry"), the see-sawing from past to present in nearly every stanza,[8] the curious logic of the narrator ("A scrap of land they have, but they Are poorest of the poor"), the pawkish humor of the rhymes ("tillage-village," "wean them-between them")—all help to undercut the sentimental. Thus the ending:

> Alas! the gratitude of men
> Has oftner left me mourning

has in context an earned substance that is not easily pathetic.

In such ways as this Wordsworth avoided current fads of genre and treatment, and of easy topicality, for a kind of poetry in *Lyrical Ballads* which was solidly original in its earthy honesty.

CHAPTER SEVEN

Wordsworth's Purpose

in the 1798 *Lyrical Ballads*

Opportunity, motivation, the various contributions of the company of Dorothy, little Basil Montagu, Thomas Poole, and Coleridge, as well as the warming and opening influence of spring, coming "slowly up that way"—all combined early in 1798 to produce a startling effect on Wordsworth's poetic activity. The change becomes apparent in Dorothy's Alfoxden Journal—a most frustrating document, since it survives only from January 20 to May 22, 1798, and that only in Knight's faulty transcription. But surely Knight would not have been likely to omit references to Wordsworth's poetic accomplishments—and one must be struck with the fact that Dorothy's entries, although themselves often poetic in their sensitive and imaginatively phrased observations, manage to go on for quite a long time without giving any indication at all that her brother was a practicing poet. She records most interestingly the look and sound of the sea, trips for bread and eggs, picking up sticks and gathering fir apples, and a great deal of walking with Coleridge. But not until March 18 does she mention William's writing any poetry: "sheltered under the hollies, during a hail-shower. The withered

leaves dance with the hailstones. William wrote a description of the storm."[1]

Thus "A Whirl-blast from Behind the Hill" was written,
or at least begun. A draft of it appears in the Alfoxden
Notebook (Reed, *CEY*, p. 227)—why it was not included in
the 1798 *Lyrical Ballads*, but waited until the 1800 edition,
is not readily apparent. The following day, however,
Dorothy recorded the start of a poem which was to be one
of Wordsworth's principal contributions to the first *Lyrical
Ballads*. "William wrote some lines describing a stunted
thorn." Mark Reed notes that a draft of lines 1—22 of "The
Thorn" appears in the Alfoxden Notebook immediately
before the draft of "A Whirl-Blast," and both seem to be
the work of one sitting, possibly indicating that Dorothy
wrote up this section of her Journal several days late—
something she apparently often did—and reversed the
order of the two poems. Possibly, but the important things
to note are their close association, and the fact that
Dorothy used as the key term for both poems Wordsworth's "describing" something. This seems to be the only
contemporary evidence as to what the poet was up to at
this time, and the only characterizing terms Dorothy used
in this part of her Journal in talking about her brother's
poetry. She does not record the fact, but just about a week
earlier in "Lines written at a small distance from my House,
and sent by my little Boy to the Person to whom they are
addressed"—which he later called "To My Sister"—William had begun by describing "the first mild day of March"
and ended by describing their attitude toward it, "It is the
hour of feeling."

It may be that critical concern with simplicity of language and subject, or with the narrative, dramatic, and
lyric elements of the *Lyrical Ballads*, has tended to obscure
this basic element of description. We recall that Hazlitt,
however, in his *Spirit of the Age*, had placed the founda-
tion of Wordsworth's originality on his descriptions: "the

author of the *Lyrical Ballads* . . . has described all these
objects in a way and with an intensity of feeling that no
one else had done before him, and has given us a new
view or aspect of nature. He is in this sense the most
original poet now living" (Howe, XI, 89). And it is
noteworthy that in July 1797, early in the intimacy that
finally produced the *Lyrical Ballads*, Coleridge wrote his
poetic epistle to Charles Lamb, "This Lime-Tree Bower my
Prison," containing some of his closest observation and
richest description. Wordsworth published in the 1798
Lyrical Ballads "Old Man Travelling, Animal Tranquility
and Decay, A Sketch," and probably between January 25
and March 5, 1798 (Reed, *CEY*, p. 27), he wrote a version
of the related "The Old Cumberland Beggar," which
appeared in the 1800 edition of *Lyrical Ballads* with the
subtitle "A Description." Possibly the character of effective
poetic description was one of the triggering factors behind
the production of the *Lyrical Ballads*. Certainly Wordsworth was thinking about the matter, and in no simplistic
way.

The final lines of the draft of "Whirl-Blast" are especially
significant in this context:

> This long description why indite?
> Because it was a pleasant sight.
>   (*PW*, II, 128)

These lines were obviously a little too flat to survive, but
they capture significantly Wordsworth's mood of the
moment at which *Lyrical Ballads* really came into being—
the idea that any sight which is pleasant or interesting
for any reason, is a fit subject for poetic description. In
fact, the function of poetry is to preserve and communicate
this interest by removing what Coleridge was to call the
"film of familiarity."[2] Wordsworth told Miss Fenwick that
the poem "The Thorn" "arose out of" his "observing,
on the ridge of Quantock Hill, on a stormy day, a thorn"

which he had "often passed in calm and bright weather without noticing it.":

I said to myself, "Cannot I by some invention do as much to make this Thorn permanently an impressive object as the storm has made it to my eyes at this moment?"[3]

The thorn was an ordinary part of the landscape, unnoticed, and apparently unpoetic, until the storm suddenly called Wordsworth's attention to it, put it in a setting of emotional response that made it poetic. This was, I believe, an exceedingly important moment in his career. What he learned, of course, was that *everything* can be poetic, if it is *perceived* poetically, *felt* poetically.

It followed that poetic treatment did not have to be artificial, Poetic with a capital P, using all the traditional devices and diction. Since description of a pleasant and interesting sight was itself important, it should be accurate, true to life, without false coloration. A suggestive insight into Wordsworth's thinking on this subject around the time of the *Lyrical Ballads* comes in his 1801 letter to Anne Taylor (*EY*, p. 328) in which, as we saw in Chapter Four, he relates to simplicity his effort to look "steadily" at his subject. He gives Miss Taylor "The Female Vagrant," which he calls "the first written of the Collection," as an example of faulty work produced *before* he had become "conscious of the importance of this rule," criticizing it as a poem in which the diction "is often vicious, and the descriptions are often false": note diction and *description*. Wordsworth cites several examples of what he means, and gives Miss Taylor some corrections. It may be particularly instructive of Wordsworth's poetic career after 1798 to look at his treatment of two lines (93-4 in the 1798 version of "The Female Vagrant"; 273-4 in the 1842 *Guilt and Sorrow*; 354-5 in Stephen Gill's reading text of *Adventures on Salisbury Plain*, 1795–c. 1799):

> But soon, with proud parade, the noisy drum
> Beat round, to sweep the streets of want and pain.

Wordsworth told Miss Taylor, "For 'with proud parade,' Read, 'day after day,' the next line For 'to *sweep* the streets' Read '*and clear'd* the streets.' " He indeed made the first change in 1805, but returned to the 1798 version from 1820; he kept the "to sweep" 1798-1832, but changed it to "to clear" by 1842. Both proposed changes are certainly aimed partly against alliteration and poetic metaphor, and partly toward descriptive accuracy. Apparently the later Wordsworth decided that "proud parade" was ironically accurate and to be preferred to the prosaic literalness of "day after day"; and finally came back to "clear" as more accurate than the metaphorical "sweep." In any event, in 1801 he was certainly thinking of accurate description as an important part of the *Lyrical Ballads* manifesto.

Descriptive accuracy, however, does not mean precise literalness. Wordsworth's own references to the eye on the object, with an assist from Coleridge's charge of "matter-of-factness,"[4] have tended to foist upon him a sort of photographic realism which was far from his intention in most of his mature work. Ultimately, he did not value *that* kind of description. Again and again from 1798 he insisted that poetry deals with the universal, general, eternal. The universalizing instrument was in different contexts the "colouring of imagination," the "inward eye," the "Mind of Man"[5]—which I think for Wordsworth had Berkeleyan overtones of the mind of God. Therefore, he repudiated on the one hand George Crabbe's kind of realistic description (what he called "mere matters of fact," about as poetical as "medical reports"), and on the other James Macpherson's false stereotyped distinctions:[6] objects, he thought, should be described *as they appeared to the fusing sensibility*; and by such means, a stunted thorn—and even a pool "three feet long and two feet wide"—could become appropriate subjects for poetry.

It ought not to be overlooked that the Advertisement to the first edition of the *Lyrical Ballads* begins, "It is the honorable characteristic of Poetry that its materials are to be found in every subject which can interest the human mind." Despite all that is said later about the language of poetry—by Wordsworth in the Advertisement and the Preface, and by reviewers and critics—the opening emphasis is on the subject matter of poetry. Wordsworth's point is that everyday subject matter has a valid human interest, relates to real human passions, and can be expressed poetically in real human language—it needs no special ornamentation of poetic language. To communicate his sense of the vitality of the thorn tree, what he sought was some "invention"—the rhetorical term is interesting—not some "decoration": he puts himself in the rhetorical school of Aristotle, not of Cicero.

Wordsworth's descriptions are not pointed simply toward the Pre-Raphaelite formula, "the poetry of the things around us," and certainly not to Ruskin's "selecting nothing."[7] Neither is Wordsworth aiming at Shelley's idyllic picture in *Prometheus Unbound* (III, iii, 30-32):

> We will entangle buds and flowers and beams
> Which twinkle on the fountain's brim, and make
> Strange combinations out of common things,

which leads to Pater's definition of the romantic as the addition of "strangeness to beauty." Wordsworth certainly insisted on selectively from among the "things around us" —not *every* subject, but every subject "which can interest the human mind," in a "selection" of the language really used by men. And his ends were not primarily either strangeness or beauty—there is nothing very lovely about swollen ankles or idiot boys. Indeed, it is remarkable how little appeal to beauty there is in Wordsworth's poems in the 1798 *Lyrical Ballads.* Although he will not insist on painting every wart or mole, he will not blink at them either, if he thinks they contribute to the substantiality that involves human feeling. Thus Wordsworth's are more "commonplace combinations of common things": the only thing that makes them strange is their context—one had not been accustomed to see such combinations in verse. What Wordsworth aimed to do in the *Lyrical Ballads* was "by some invention" of narrative, character, and setting, to charge the commonplace with feeling.

Later in the Advertisement, Wordsworth says that "Goody Blake and Harry Gill" was "founded on a well-authenticated fact which happened in Warwickshire." He thinks it proper to add that the other poems in the group are "either absolute inventions of the author, or facts which took place within his personal observation or that of his friends." Significantly, he appears to make no value distinctions between those poems which were based on actual events and those which he invented. The important thing to him, it would appear, was the essential verity of the human feeling, not the literal historicity of the action. Coleridge's oft-quoted contemporary remark to Hazlitt about Wordsworth's "matter-of-factness" applies obviously to his detailed verisimilitude and earthy substantiality, not to factual literalness. So long as the poem was about something that could be seen and felt, that was true to human nature, it did not seem to matter whether it had in actual fact happened just as described. What was essential was the description of someone seeing and feeling. Later, in the Preface to his 1815 edition, Wordsworth listed as first among the "powers requisite for the production of poetry" those "of Observation and Description." Such powers are not enough in themselves, he makes clear, for they are essentially passive—but they are indispensable. He summed up the relation of language to observation in his 1800 Preface: "I have at all times endeavoured to look steadily at my subject; consequently, there is I hope in these Poems little falsehood of description, and my ideas are expressed in language fitted to their respective importance." But the significant point, that which he felt distinguished his poems "from the popular Poetry of the day," was not the language or even the subjects described, but that "the feeling therein developed gives importance to the action and situation, and not the action and situation to the feeling."[8]

Keeping his eye on his object was, of course, not new to Wordsworth. As early as "The Vale of Esthwaite" he had drawn upon accurate observation; and he told Miss Fenwick that in *An Evening Walk*, his first published major poem, there was not an image which he had not observed. In these early poems, however, he had not used a "language fitted to their respective importance," but had depended for his heightening effects largely upon poetic diction, personification, inversion, and other devices of ornamentation. Furthermore, his motivation then had been more nearly photographic. He cites to Miss Fenwick as an example of his close observation in *An Evening Walk* the following lines:

> And, fronting the bright west, yon oak entwines
> Its darkening boughs and leaves in stronger lines.
>   (214-15 *cf.* "Vale of Esthwaite," 97-8)

The moment he perceived this image, he goes on, "was important in my poetical history; for I date from it my consciousness of the infinite variety of natural appearances which had been unnoticed by the poets of any age or country, so far as I was acquainted with them; and I made a resolution to supply, in some degree, the deficiency" (*PW*, I, 319). This is an impulse to broaden the poetic range of representational accuracy by an eye keen for light and shadow. But Wordsworth's resolve here is merely to present an image, not invent anything to impress it upon the reader's mind or connect it with human feelings. The *Lyrical Ballads* impulse was clearly different.

By 1798 Wordsworth had taken another step important to his "poetical history"; he had definitely moved beyond this pictorial stage of *An Evening Walk* to a much more sophisticated kind of description based on an almost

mystical awareness of an interaction in observation between the scene and the observer, so that the quality of the
experience became the significant thing ("It is the hour of
feeling"), and the feeling gave importance to the action.
When in 1843 he looked back over his poetic career,
Wordsworth declared that "no change" had taken place in
his poetic "manner" for the last forty-five years.[9] The Great
Divide was obviously at the 1798 *Lyrical Ballads*. We can
only speculate as to what he was thinking about: was the
essence of the "change" the plain language, the commonplace subjects, the primacy of feelings—of the combination
of the whole under some Wordsworthian rubric like the
eternal and the inevitable? Probably the latter in Wordsworth's thinking, but the really important shift seems to
have been in the direction of concern with the psychology
of feelings, toward finding devices for concreticizing or—as
it were—providing "objective correlatives" for feelings.

In the Alfoxden Notebook are the following interesting
lines, probably written in March 1798,[10] which perhaps
represent a sort of transitional state in the change in poetic
manner:

> to gaze
> On that green hill and on those scattered trees
> And feel a pleasant consciousness of life
> In the impression of that loveliness
> Until the sweet sensation called the mind
> Into itself, by image from without
> Unvisited, and all her reflex powers
> Wrapped in a still dream [of] forgetfulness.
>
> I lived without the knowledge that I lived
> Then by those beauteous forms brought back again
> To lose myself again as if my life
> Did ebb and flow with a strange mystery.
>
> (*PW*, V, 341)

The conception in these lines is obviously close to the idea
expressed in "Lines Written a few miles above Tintern
Abbey,"

> we are laid asleep
> In body, and become a living soul:
> (46-47)

Wordsworth is here dealing with the mystery of creative perception in a philosophical way. He is telling us that observation is profound and transcendent, but in the Alfoxden Notebook lines he is not showing us; he is expounding his feeling, not making us feel it. The "green hill" and "scattered trees" of the fragment are like the thorn in sunshine—they need something to make them vivid and concrete so that they enter into our consciousness. They need to be connected with some incident, dramatized so that we can share the poet's feelings, or understand and possibly identify with characters who project the feelings.

Wordsworth's insight about the stunted thorn is an insight in this direction, a fresh perception of poetic reality. The essence of his *An Evening Walk* comment is that poetry is observation and description; in his 1800-1805 note to "The Thorn," however, he vitalizes the description: "For the Reader cannot be too often reminded that Poetry is passion: it is the history or science of feelings."[11] These feelings, these passions, have power, however, only as they are firmly attached to and derive from vivid descriptions—not pictorial or photographic, but generally and universally internalized. In the note to "The Thorn," Wordsworth explained: "I had two objects to attain; first, to represent a picture which should not be unimpressive, yet consistent with the character that should describe it; secondly, while I adhered to the style in which such persons describe, to take care that words, which in their minds are impregnated with passion, should likewise convey passion to Readers who are not accustomed to sympathize with men feeling in that manner or using such language" (*PW*, II, 512). What this boils down to is a *picture* which is impressive by reason of being "impregnated" with communicable passions. As Wordsworth put it in his 1815

"Essay, Supplementary to the Preface," the privilege and duty of poetry is "to treat of things not as they *are*, but as they *appear*; not as they exist in themselves, but as they *seem* to exist to the *senses*, and the *passions*" (*Prose Wks.*, III, 63).

My guess is that in early March 1798, spurred on to write more poetry for financial reasons, and finding himself improving in his poetic facility, Wordsworth got the idea of writing a number of short poems which did not simply see and describe, but created people seeing and describing, so as to bring in the history of feelings. Such poems were not to be formal and hortatory, as the earlier "Lines Left upon a Seat in a Yew Tree" had been, but direct and natural in the language of observing personae. We remember that Coleridge in his *Biographia Literaria* statement said that Wordsworth added two or three poems written in "his own character," implying that most of those designed for *Lyrical Ballads* were in some other character.[12] Coleridge quotes Wordsworth in 1800 as wishing that Bürger would make the reader forget him "in his creations," and going on to say, "It seems to me, that in poems descriptive of human nature, however short they may be, character is absolutely necessary, &c.: incidents are among the lowest allurements of poetry."[13]

This comment on Bürger suggests what the poems of the 1798 period confirm, that the sort of invention Wordsworth valued most was not simply of incident, but of incident which revealed character. One of these poems he called "Anecdote for Fathers," and many of them are anecdotal. They describe an event, usually without enough sequence to have much narrative element, but with some psychological interest. They deal with character not in the picturesque sense of an unique character, but in the universal sense of a typical character with whose feelings

all sensitive readers can empathize. In his 1800-1805 note
to "The Thorn" he makes the point, "The character which
I have here introduced speaking is sufficiently common"
(*PW*, II, 512). We remember again that Coleridge said in
the *Biographia Literaria* comment that for Wordsworth's
poems "the characters and incidents were to be such, as
will be found in every village and its vicinity, where there
is a meditative and feeling mind to seek after them, or
to notice them, when they present themselves" (*Biog. Lit.*,
II, 5). And although there is often an undifferentiated
spokesman called "I," he is frequently either not important
as an individual or not particularly William Wordsworth—
he is the observer, notable not for himself, but for what
he sees and feels; he is the "meditative and feeling
mind." The impulse is not simply, or perhaps even
primarily, dramatic, although there is a considerable dramatic element, as Stephen Parrish has well shown. By the
time Wordsworth wrote the Preface to his 1815 *Poems*,
he recognized a difference between "enthusiastic and meditative Imagination, of poetical, as contra-distinguished
from human and dramatic Imagination."[14] This remark
seems to mean that the dramatic is not poetical, or at
least not as poetical as the meditative. I suspect that Wordsworth believed this in 1798. In MS B of *The Borderers*,
which probably represents a text of November 1797 (*PW*,
I, 344; Reed, *CEY*, 330), occur the famous lines which
Wordsworth prefaced to *The White Doe of Rylstone*:

> Action is transitory—a step, a blow
> . . . .
> Suffering is permanent, obscure and dark,
> And has [shares *MS C on*] the nature of infinity.
>   (III, 1539, 1543-4)

What Wordsworth was trying to do in 1798 was to see
freshly and describe vividly by presenting actions and
situations which incorporated sufferings and feelings that

were not transitory, of characters who were sort of objective correlatives for eternal humanity. They are, therefore,
almost archtypes: Harry Gill is avarice and superstition,
Simon Lee is impotent old age. The "Mad Mother" and
the little maid of "We Are Seven," the speaker in "The
Last of the Flock" are not even given names: they represent
maternity or childhood or man's relationship to property.

In a passage which appeared in the 1800 Preface, and
with some modification through 1836, but was cut from the
1850 version and is therefore not so well known as it
might be, Wordsworth is a little more explicit about his
purpose in the *Lyrical Ballads*:

But speaking in less general language, it is to follow the fluxes
and refluxes of the mind when agitated by the great and simple
affections of our nature. This object I have endeavoured in these
short essays to attain by various means; by tracing the maternal
passion through many of its more subtle windings, as in the poems
of the IDIOT BOY and the MAD MOTHER; by accompanying the last
struggles of a human being at the approach of death, cleaving
in solitude to life and society, as in the Poem of the FORSAKEN INDIAN;
by shewing, as in the Stanzas entitled WE ARE SEVEN, the perplexity
and obscurity which in childhood attend our notion of death,
or rather our utter inability to admit that notion; or by displaying
the strength of fraternal, or to speak more philosophically, of
moral attachment when early associated with the great and beautiful objects of nature, as in THE BROTHERS; or, as in the Incident of
SIMON LEE, by placing my Reader in the way of receiving from
ordinary moral sensations another and more salutary impression
than we are accustomed to receive from them. It has also been part
of my general purpose to attempt to sketch characters under the
influence of less impassioned feelings, as in the OLD MAN TRAVELLING,
THE TWO THIEVES, &c. characters of which the elements are simple,
belonging rather to nature than to manners, such as exist now and
will probably always exist, and which from their constitution
may be distinctly and profitably contemplated. (*Prose Wks.*,
I, 126, 128)

It is interesting to speculate as to why Wordsworth chose
these particular poems as examples of his purpose "to

follow the fluxes and refluxes of the mind." All but two—
"The Brothers" and "The Two Thieves"—are in the 1798
edition; and all but "The Brothers" and "Old Man Travelling," which are in blank verse, are in lyrical stanzas and
probably were counted among the *Lyrical Ballads* rather
than the "Few Other Poems." Certainly the poems Wordsworth cites are very different from each other, and perhaps
were chosen to underline the "various means" he says he
uses to attain his ends, and possibly calculated *ex post facto*
to claim a unity for the varied collection. Two of the
themes which he picks out—motherhood and death—are
obviously connected with "the great and simple affections
of our nature." "Simon Lee" is more obscurely classified as
providing a "salutary impression" from "ordinary moral
sensations"; and "Old Man Travelling" and "The Two
Thieves" are clearly in a different category of poems
which "attempt to sketch characters under the influence
of less impassioned feelings." Since all of the poems
mentioned sketch characters under the influence of feelings, the difference in the two classifications appears
to have been between impassioned and less impassioned.

"The Old Man Travelling"—to focus on the 1798
examples—is probably one of the earlier poems in the
collection (Reed dates it "between the latter half of 1796
and early June 1797 inclusive"), but it is clearly related
to the descriptive impulse of the *Lyrical Ballads*. Wordsworth told Miss Fenwick that this poem was "an overflow-
ing from the Old Cumberland Beggar"—which is subtitled
"A Description"—and the manuscripts bear him out (Reed,
CEY, p. 342). The feelings of the "Old Man Travelling"
seem, as is clear from the 1798 version, to be similar in
character to those informing the examples of more impassioned feelings: he is a father travelling to the bedside of
his dying son. From 1815 the last six lines, which provide
this information, were dropped, and the aged traveller is

presented as an image of "settled quiet," an object lesson of a peace which literally "passeth understanding." The feelings are less impassioned, not because they are any less profound, but because they are more tranquil. It is worth noting that there is no dialogue in this poem, no sense of immediacy, no struggle—"all effort seems forgotten."

These lines reflect the stoic stance of "Peele Castle" and other poems which have been judged to reflect Wordsworth's mood after the death of his brother John in 1805. Because the situation of "passion spent" is relatively static, it seems to lend itself to the descriptive mode. The Old Man is indeed travelling, but he moves so quietly that he does not even disturb the "little hedge-row birds, / That peck along the road." There is an almost frozen unity about him: "in his face, his step, / His gait, is one expression." The economy of Wordsworth's sketch is remarkable; every detail contributes until the reader like the Old Man is "insensibly subdued." But the description is not pictorial in the same sense as that of the oak entangling its "darkening boughs." Wordsworth's subject here is human relationship; he is describing a pattern of feelings. The Old Man has the resonance of a symbol. The key note is permanence even in decay: "belonging rather to nature than to manners, such as exists now and will probably always exist."

It is also worth observing that even those poems in the *Lyrical Ballads* which have a narrative element are largely a series of tableaus. Wordsworth called for an "invention" to make the thorn memorable, but the really vivid passages in the poem are descriptive. And in 1809 when he wrote to Coleridge about an appropriate organization for his collected poems, he placed "The Thorn" in a climactic position in a class of poems "interesting to a meditative or imaginative mind either from the moral importance of the *pictures* [my *italics*] or from the employment they give to the understanding" (MY, I, 335). The poem begins with an impressionistic picture of the thorn, how it "looks" to an observing "you":

> There is a thorn; it looks so old,
> In truth you'd find it hard to say,
> How it could every have been young,
> It looks so old and grey.
> Not higher than a two-years' child,
> It stands erect this aged thorn;
> No leaves it has, no thorny points;
> It is a mass of knotted joints,
> A wretched thing forlorn.
> It stands erect, and like a stone
> With lichens it is overgrown.
>
>   (1—11)

Of course the garrulous retired sea-captain tells a sort of hearsay tale, but the vivid bits are the descriptions of the "beauteous heap," the hill of moss; of the "jutting crag" which turned out to be "A woman seated on the ground" (198). Wordsworth felt so strongly about detailed, accurate-sounding description that from 1798 through 1815 he clung to the ridiculed lines about the little pond:

> I've measured it from side to side:
> 'Tis three feet long, and two feet wide
>
>   (32-3)

which he finally relinquished in the 1820 edition, although still protesting to Crabb Robinson that they "ought to be liked."[15]

The descriptive mode is existential; it describes a state of being: "There is a thorn." Coleridge had done the same thing in the poem which keyed the *Lyrical Ballads*: "It is an ancyent Marinere." And Wordsworth in other poems: "it is the first mild day of March" ("Lines written at a small distance" ["To My Sister"],1). We are reminded that in the early version of his famous dedicatory experience while walking home from an all-night dance during his first Long Vacation (1788) he wrote:

> Magnificent
> The morning *was*, in memorable pomp,
> More glorious than I ever had beheld,
> The Sea *was* laughing at a distance; all
> The solid Mountains *were* as bright as clouds,
> (Prelude, A, IV, 330-4)

The italicized forms of the verb *to be* (my italics) were in the 1850 version changed—and probably for the better—to "rose," "lay" and "shone" respectively. The A version, however, reflects the curious emphasis on simply *being* which, as we have seen, Wordsworth expressed in his 1802 letter to Sara Hutchinson about "Resolution and Independence":

What is brought forward? "A lonely place, a Pond" "by which an old man *was*, far from all house or home"—not stood, not sat, but "*was*"—the figure presented in the most naked simplicity possible. (*EY*, p. 366)

It is also worth noting here that in his moving description of his early religious feelings, in the second book of *The Prelude*, he speaks of conversing "With things that really are" (A II, 413) and feels "the sentiment of Being spread / O'er all that moves, and all that seemeth still" (A II, 420-1). The language is characteristically existential, and the mode is statically descriptive.

CHAPTER EIGHT

What Is a "Lyrical Ballad"?

Why Wordsworth and Coleridge elected to call the collection of poems they published in 1798 "lyrical ballads" is one of the interesting and probably finally unanswerable questions of literary history. The *British Critic* reviewer of the 1800 edition understandably complained, "The title of the Poems is in some degree, objectionable; for what Ballads are not *lyrical*?[1] It has more recently been suggested that the essential quality of a lyrical as opposed to any other kind of ballad is subjectivity (Campbell and Mueschke) and the dramatic (Parrish).[2] Undoubtedly, there is some truth in both interpretations; Wordsworth was, as we have seen, concerned with feelings that gave importance to the narrative line, rather than the other way around. And he tended to dramatize the feelings to make them vivid and memorable—like his thorn tree. Yet when he objects to Bürger's not losing himself in "his creations," he does not seem to be asking for subjectivity, although he may be calling for individual characters in dramatic situations. This commentary on Bürger ends, however, "I love his *'Tra ra la'* dearly; but less of the horn and more of the lute—and far, far more of the pencil."[3] The pencil and the lute suggest that Wordsworth thought ballads should be descriptive and lyrical. In his 1815 Preface he puts ballads—along with hymns, odes, elegies and songs—in the class of "the lyrical," poems which require "for the production of their *full* effect, an accompaniment of music." (*PW*, II, 433; *Prose Wks.*, III, 27).

Such a classification was, as Paul Sheats points out, received wisdom—made in Knox's *Elegant Extracts*, the anthology used by Wordsworth at Hawkshead School, and by John Aikin in his *Essay on Songwriting* (1772).[4] Indeed, even today a "ballad" is a synonym for a song, usually carrying a burden of easily accessible feeling.

As far as I know, neither of the authors of this curiously titled little volume explained in any document that has survived exactly what they had in mind by the famous designation. That they meant something specific by their title, and did not use it facilely as just a convenient conglomerate, an unusual synonym for "poems," is indicated by its last part: "With a Few Other Poems." Clearly some, indeed most, of the contents were thus specifically designated as a particular kind of ballad, distinguishable from "other poems." Yet the title seems not to have been of very great importance to Wordsworth, because by 1800 he was reportedly ready to give it up rather easily. Dorothy explains to her friend Jane Marshall in a letter of September 10, 1800:

My Brother William is going to publish a second Edition of the Lyrical Ballads with a second volume. He intends to give them the title of "Poems by W. Wordsworth" as Mrs. Robinson has claimed the title and is about publishing a volume of *Lyrical Tales*. This is a great objection to the former title, particularly as they are both printed at the same press and Longman is the publisher of both the works. (*EY*, p. 297)

An interesting aspect of the statement is that Dorothy at least, and presumably William also, considered that in the public eye "ballads" and "tales" were synonymous.

Of course it is possible that Wordsworth was willing enough to give up the title of *Lyrical Ballads* because the nomenclature was not his to begin with, but Coleridge's. If we can take literally words Landor puts in his own mouth in his *Imaginary Conversation* "Archdeacon Hare and Walter Landor" (1853), Wordsworth came to regret the title, just as he came to regret the Preface which Coleridge persuaded him to write:[5]

Your friend Wordsworth was induced to divide his minor Poems under the separate head of these two [Fancy and Imagination]; probably at the suggestion of Coleridge, who persuaded him, as he himself told me, to adopt the name of *Lyrical Ballads*. He was sorry, he said, that he took the advice. And well he might be; for *lyre* and *ballad* belong not to the same age or the same people.

As far as I know, the closest Wordsworth came to revealing what he meant by "lyrical ballad" appears in a remark in a passage of the 1800 Preface which was dropped out after 1836. He was discussing the psychological truth embodied in "Goody Blake and Harry Gill": "And I have the satisfaction of knowing that it has been communicated to many hundreds of people who would never have heard of it, had it not been narrated as a Ballad, and in a more impressive meter than is usual in Ballads."[6] This poem is a short tale: it has the subtitle "A True Story." And it employs an eight-line stanza, usually rhyming *a, b, a, b, c, d, c, d,* but occasionally repeating the *b* rhyme, and regularly using a feminine rhyme in the *a* position—rather more "impressive" than is characteristic of either folk ballads or street ballads. It is noteworthy that Wordsworth wrote Coleridge (*EY,* p. 234) late in 1798 about Bürger's work, making it clear that they agreed in valuing particularly the German's versification—Wordsworth especially the "delicious and *pathetic* effect" of the double rhymes. This is "impressive meter," which sets a ballad apart.

Wordsworth makes special reference to his metrical strategy also in the already cited 1800-1805 note to "The Thorn," in which he explains that the poem ought to have been equipped with an introductory poem describing the narrator, and continues:

It was my wish in this poem to shew the manner in which such men cleave to the same ideas; and to follow the turns of passion, always different, yet not palpably different, by which their conversation is swayed. . . . It seemed to me that this might be done by calling in the assistance of Lyrical and rapid Metre. It was necessary that the Poem, to be natural, should in reality move slowly; yet I hoped that, by the aid of the metre, to those who should at all enter into the spirit of the Poem, it would appear to move quickly. (*PW*, II, 512-13)

"The Thorn" is a rather wordy poem, and we may question whether Wordsworth's metric scheme succeeds in making its 253 lines appear to move quickly. His problem here is the difficult one of how to write about, and from the mind of, dull people, without being dull. Possibly he put too much dependence on the metrical devices. But we can see what he was trying to do with the 11-line stanza which is speeded up at two points by triplet lines and also accelerated by the throw-away effect of the unrhymed third and fifth lines, and the snapping together effect of two couplets, including a final couplet that often employs feminine rhymes—which may be thought to produce a tripping quality:

$$4 \ 4 \ 4 \ 3 \ 4 \ 4 \ 4 \ 4 \ 3 \ 4 \ 4$$
$$a \ b \ c \ b \ d \ e \ f \ f \ e \ g \ g$$

At any rate, we can understand how this varied music could be called a "lyrical ballad."

Probably the germ of the idea of a sub-genre of metrically superior ballads was Coleridge's "The Ancient Mariner," which used variations upon the ballad quatrain by putting in occasional internal rhyme and five-line stanzas. This poem, as we have seen, was apparently referred to

among the collaborators as Coleridge's "ballad," and its
metrical sophistication allowed it to be called a "lyrical"
one. Significantly, however, "The Three Graves," another
ballad—but metrically simpler and cruder—which in some
way not quite clear was composed between Wordsworth
and Coleridge in 1798[7] and which would seem to fit both
the collaborative effort and the curse motif, which we have
seen may at one time have been a unifying element to the
collection, was *not* put in *Lyrical Ballads*. Coleridge published parts III and IV of "The Three Graves" in 1809 in
The Friend, and in 1817 in *Sibylline Leaves*; in prefatory
remarks to the latter appearance he apologizes:

The language was intended to be dramatic; that is, suited to the
narrator; and the metre corresponds to the homeliness of the
diction. It is therefore presented as the fragment, not of a Poem,
but of a common Ballad-tale.

According to E.H. Coleridge, the MS reads, "in the common ballad metre" (*Poems*, p. 267n). It would appear,
therefore, that what is important in making a "lyrical
ballad" is not the dramatic so much as the metrical
sophistication—this piece is a ballad tale, in the common
ballad metre, and not even worthy of being called poetry;
it is evidently not a "lyrical" ballad.

Only five of the poems by Wordsworth in the 1798
edition are in unvaried ballad meter (*a, b, a, b*): "Lines
written at a small distance," "Anecdote for Fathers," "Lines
written in early spring" and the paired "Expostulation
and Reply" and "The Tables Turned." None of these is
very long; the longer pieces, and those which Wordsworth's and Coleridge's comments suggest they most valued, employ more sophisticated stanzaic patterns.

"The Mad Mother," has a 10-line stanza somewhat
similar to the 11-line verse of "The Thorn," but interestingly different. The shorter poem uses a more monotonous pattern, with three couplets to the stanza, predomi-
nantly tetrameter, and never employing feminine rhymes

(*a, a, b, b, c, d, c, d, e, e*). Perhaps Wordsworth considered that the less varied form was more appropriate to the mania of the speaker. According to Coleridge, the popular actress Mrs. Jordan was planning to *sing* stanzas from this poem as Cora in Sheridan's *Pizarro* (*Letters*, I, 654)— obviously a *lyrical ballad.*

Apparently, however, Wordsworth and Coleridge did not think of themselves as inventing an important new species of verse, or they would hardly have said so little about it, especially since they had such a made-to-order opportunity as that afforded by the Preface to the 1800 edition; and Wordsworth would scarcely have been willing to give up the title so easily to "Perdita" Robinson's rough synonym. It is more likely that they were just seeking a novel and descriptive title for their little book, a title which would at the same time be different from those attached to run-of-the-mill collections of verse, and also would take advantage of the current popularity of ballads.

Simply "poems" was, of course, neither original nor eye-catching. Of the collections of verse published in 1798, most of them were called "poems" of some sort. Four were named *Poems on Various Subjects* (by Mary Ann Chantrell, A Lady, R. Anderson, and Eliza Daye), and there were the variants of Hannah Brand's *Plays and Poems,* and the Rev. Benjamin Johnson's *Original Poems.* "Lyrical," however, suggested—as Wordsworth and Coleridge clearly intended that it should—some superior excellence in the versification. The *Critical Review* in a February 1798 comment on Thomas Townshend's *Poems* (1797) declared: "Of all classes of poetry the lyric is perhaps the most difficult. Few writers are capable of producing the rapid combinations, the precipitation of spirit, which it requires; and these beauties are not of a nature to be generally admired or understood" (XXII, 186). Although W.L. Bowles called a small volume *Song of the Battle of the*

Nile (1799), he explained in a footnote: "I need not say that Song, in this place, is used in its highest sense, as a Lyrical composition" (p. 13). Something of the same sort of snobbery was perhaps responsible for William Smyth's calling his poems, a second edition of which appeared in 1798, *English Lyrics*. And for Southey's labeling a section of his *Poems* (1797) "Lyric Poems," and asking Cottle that in the printing the section be given a black-letter title page.[8] Probably also for "Perdita" Robinson's choosing *Lyrical Tales* as a title for her 1800 collection.

By "lyrical" ballads, therefore, Wordsworth and Coleridge probably meant "superior" ballads. Like the prophet Amos separating himself from the orgiastic "Sons of the Prophets," Wordsworth was putting himself above the average balladmonger, who might pretend to no more than cobbling a bit of doggerel to exploit a current sensational crime. Even J. Bisset, a very ordinary versifier, author of *A Poetic Survey round Birmingham . . . Accompanied by a Magnificent Directory* (1800)—in the Introduction to which he confessed accurately, "My pen, I fear, will never raise my fame"—nevertheless apologized the next year when he published *A Peace Offering, Songs*, declaring in his preface, "The Author of the MAGNIFICENT and GRAND NATIONAL DIRECTORY, is not at all ambitious in coming before the Public, as 'a Ballad Writer' " (p. v).

Undoubtedly, since as we have seen Wordsworth made much of feeling in his comments on these poems, by a "lyrical ballad" he must have meant not only one that was metrically superior, but also one which bore some of the emotional charge that is commonly connected with lyricism; as Ruskin put it, "Lyric poetry is the expression by the poet of his own feelings."[9] Although the feelings of the *Lyrical Ballads* may have been, and probably were, Wordsworth's own, he—as we have noted—was not concerned to present them personally. The universality of the feeling, the typicality of the situation, were important, not the particular individuals involved. But the association of lyric poetry and feelings was probably as direct for Wordsworth and Coleridge as it was for Ruskin.

And this association with strong feelings had for Wordsworth significant implications concerning style. He believed that when people were under the influence of strong emotions they had difficulty in organizing their ideas and in expressing themselves—language literally failed. Therefore they stammered, repeated themselves, spoke and thought in an abrupt and jerky, almost illogical fashion. This belief explains a great deal about the diction and syntax of the *Lyrical Ballads*.

Wordsworth specifically defends tautology in his 1800-1805 note to "The Thorn":

> now every man must know that an attempt is rarely made to communicate impassioned feelings without something of an accompanying consciousness of the inadequateness of our own powers, or the deficiencies of language. During such efforts there will be a craving in the mind, and as long as it is unsatisfied the Speaker will cling to the same words, or words of the same character. (*PW*, II, 513)

Whether or not passion plucks "berries from the myrtle and the ivy" (as Samuel Johnson denied), Wordsworth obviously did not believe it supported the luxury of synonyms. Rather, the mind clings repetitiously to the same words—not only because of verbal poverty or a kind of primordial simplicity which precludes playing with alternative forms, but because of a special solace in the friendly echo. There is something more in Wordsworth's conception than the point Ezra Pound makes in a letter to Harriet Monroe (January 1915): "When one really thinks and feels one stammers with simple speech."[10] Wordsworth continues in his note on "The Thorn":

> There are also various other reasons why repetition and apparent tautology are frequently beauties of the highest kind. Among the chief of these reasons is the interest which the mind attaches to

words, not only as symbols of the passion, but as *things*, active and efficient, which are of themselves part of the passion. And further, from a spirit of fondness, exultation, and gratitude, the mind luxuriates in the repetition of words which appear successfully to communicate its feelings. (*PW*, II, 513)

The language of a "lyrical ballad" is, therefore not exactly—as Roger Sharrock seems to suggest in his penetrating essay on "Wordsworth's Revolt against Literature"[11]—the product of anti-literary pessimism, a diction of despair born of some sort of revolt against art; rather its presents the mind's luxuriating in words as a form of art, albeit a less artificial and more natural form of art than the more sophisticated view which automatically eschewed tautology. In times of emotional stress words become talismans, and take on an almost ritualistic quality. We know that they do in chanting and keening. Wordsworth extended the terrain to "lyrical ballads." His theory of language here is almost mystical, in part irrational. In the definition of a poet which Wordsworth added to the Preface in 1802 he declared, "no words, which *his* fancy or imagination can suggest, will be to be compared with those which are the emanations of reality and truth" (*Prose Wks.*, I, 139).

Lyrical Ballads, then, are finely crafted songs of popular feeling; and there is a tension between the relatively elaborate metrical devices which make them more lyrical and more impressive songs, and the natural diction and syntax which are the "emanations of truth and reality" from deeply felt and universal emotions and therefore at least appear less artful—or at any rate, less artificial. This tension is one of the reasons the collection was innovative in its time and remains somewhat awkward in ours. Paul Sheats has quite properly insisted that the *Lyrical Ballads* are "presentations of pre-selected artistic forms to an audience for the sake of highly complex and premeditated effects," and other critics have called attention to sophisticated artistry; for instance Albert S. Gérard in his analysis of the "overall polarity of positive and negative elements that constitute the structural axis" of "The Thorn."[12] But these effects are usually conveyed in the language of some spokesman whose strong feelings are vouched for by relatively uncouth language.

The tautology which Wordsworth is defensive about in "The Thorn" is not so conspicuous in his other poems in the collection. There are a few passages like these lines (11—12) from "We Are Seven":

> Her eyes were fair, and very fair,
> —Her beauty made me glad,

in which words and ideas are repeated in a rather simple-minded fashion. More generally distributed among the poems is the disjointed syntactic trick of repeating the subject of a sentence or an objective complement in noun and pronoun form.[13] The archetypical example is "The eye it cannot chuse but see" ("Expostulation and Reply," 17). But variations on the device are fairly common; some examples:

> And every man I chanc'd to see,
> I thought he knew some ill of me ("The Last of the Flock," 73-4)

> Alas! 'tis very little, all
> Which they can do between them ("Simon Lee," 55-6)

> Thy lips I feel them, baby! they ("The Mad Mother," 33)

> His heart it was so full of glee ("The Idiot Boy", 92)

> And Susan she begins to fear ("The Idiot Boy", 187)

Apparently Wordsworth believed that people in a state of strong feelings did not think their sentences out, and therefore fell into various awkward repetitions which comfortingly struck through to things as they *are*. His is a kind of linguistic existentialism. We are reminded of Heideggar's views on language. As William Barrett put it:

Language, for Heidegger, is not primarily a system of sounds or of marks on paper symbolizing those sounds. Sounds and marks upon paper can become language only because man, insofar as he exists, stands within language. This looks very paradoxical; but, as with the rest of Heidegger, to understand what he means we have to cast off our usual habits of thoughts and let ourselves see what the thing is—i.e., let the thing itself be seen rather than riding roughshod over it with ready-made conceptions.[14]

From all this, the combination *Lyrical Ballads* appears to have been from different points of view both tautological and somewhat paradoxical; it probably covered intentionally a broad spectrum. If "lyrical" connoted natural feeling, expressed in song of excellence, and thereby at least metrical sophistication, then "ballad" besides echoing "song" suggested a certain folk simplicity and popular narrative element. A great variety of ballads and tales were being published at the end of the eighteenth century, and evidently were being bought. It is significant that Longman apparently would not let Wordsworth change the title of the second edition of *Lyrical Ballads* to "Poems by W. Wordsworth," and that when the 1805 edition appeared it was announced in the *Monthly Advertiser* as "Wordsworth's Ballads. . . . The Fourth Edition of LYRICAL BALLADS; with Pastoral and other Poems. By W. Wordsworth."[15]

The notion of a special kind of ballads would not have seemed strange to contemporary readers: qualifying titles were frequent. J.C. Cross in his *Parnassian Bagatelles* (1796) included two "pastoral ballads" and an "elegiac ballad." John Wolcot (Peter Pindar) also made the latter combination in *Pindariana* (1794), which contains "The Song of Disappointment; An Elegiac Ballad." George Huddesford's *Poems* (1801) reprinted his "The Renowned

History and Rare Achievements of John Wilkes. An Heroic Ballad," and Thomas Dibdin even produced *St. David's Day: or, the Honest Welshman. A Ballad Farce* (1801).

The word "ballad" in the title probably had for Wordsworth and Coleridge's contemporaries two interesting implications—a flavor of primitive antiquity, and a suggestion of a basis in fact. Note, for instance, that Thomas Hull included "The Tale of Foscue. Written in Imitation of the Old English Ballad" and "The Unconscious Avenger . . . In the ancient ballad style" among his *Moral Tales in Verse, Founded on Real Events* (1797). Similarly, Mrs. Grant published "A Ballad, founded on fact" in *Poems on Various Subjects* (1803), and James Fordyce in his *Poems* (1786) notes that "Love and Grief: A Ballad" is "written in imitation of the ancient British Poetry, and founded on the strictest truth." Mary Robinson stresses the antiquity and simplicity, and introduces a collection of tales, which includes an imitation of Spenser, with this: "The following little Poems are written after the Model of the Old English Ballads, and are inscribed to those who admire the simplicity of that kind of versification." So Dr. Burney in his review of the *Lyrical Ballads* does not appear to recognize Wordsworth's "impressive metre," but rather exaggerates the antiquity, objecting to a class of poetry "cultivated at the expense of a higher species of versification, unknown in our language at the time when the elder writers, whom this author condescends to imitate," wrote their ballads.[16] George Davies Harley emphasized the factual and simple in his *Ballad Stories, Sonnets, &c.* (1799), which carried the epigraph:

> The simple Fact, the Gossip's Tale,
> And Wild-Flowers gather'd in the Vale.

Wordsworth himself played down the ancient quality, saying in his Advertisement: "The Rime of the Ancyent Marinere was professedly written in imitation of the *style*,

as well as the spirit of the elder poets; but with a few
exceptions, the Author believes that the language adopted
in it has been equally intelligible for these three last
centuries." However, he emphasizes, as we remember, that
"The Tale of Goody Blake and Harry Gill is founded on
a well-authenticated fact which happened in Warwickshire" and others of the poems are from "facts which took
place within his personal observation or that of his
friends." Apparently, for Wordsworth "ballad" did not
necessarily connote antiquity, except perhaps in so far as
that suggested universality, perservering reality. It is obvious enough that the exotic romanticism of "Ancient Mariner" is not characteristic of the *Lyrical Ballads*, but it
should be noted also that Wordsworth did not appreciate
that quality, and for his part of the volume deliberately
eschewed it. He even considered dropping Coleridge's
famous ballad from the second edition, and apologized
rather ungraciously for its faults in a prefatory note which
he later dropped.[17]

Thus we have the paradoxical situation that Coleridge's
"ballad," the particular piece of superior balladry which
probably started the collection and had most to do with the
choice of the title "Lyrical Ballads," was not characteristic
of the volume as it developed, or representative of Wordsworth's purpose in 1798. His archetypal poem is "Goody
Blake and Harry Gill," a piece of descriptive narrative in
"impressive meter" which makes real in the hearts of men
a little tale about elemental people, a tale concerning
which the feeling gives importance to the action.

Probably it is not fruitful to try to find anything any
more substantive as vital to the definition of a "lyrical
ballad." Albert Gérard has suggested that the *Lyrical
Ballads* reveal that Wordsworth was "chiefly moved by the
evil present in the human condition."[18] Such a conclusion
is understandable, but perhaps one-sided. We have already

observed the insistent emphasis on "joy" in the poems, and have noted in passing but perhaps should call attention to the play of humor: the rich burlesque and mock epic elements of "The Idiot Boy,"[19] the sympathetic humor of "Simon Lee," the magisterial frolicsomeness of "Anecdote for Fathers" and "We Are Seven," the humorous geniality of "Expostulation and Reply" and "The Tables Turned," and even the macabre humor of "Goody Blake and Harry Gill." It is therefore perhaps fairer to say that Wordsworth participated in the wisdom of Horace Walpole's famous *mot*: "The world is a comedy to those that think, a tragedy to those who feel" (ltr. to Sir Horace Mann [1742])—and did both.

If there is any thematic unity to the poems which can be called "lyrical ballads," it is probably not a curse motif or the "evil present in the human condition," nor even simply the "human condition." We remember that although "Lines Written in Early Spring" (7-8) echoes:

> And much it griev'd my heart to think
> What man has made of man,

the poem rises from the conviction that "every flower / Enjoys the air it breathes" (11-12), and the sense of pleasure in nature is important because:

> To her fair works did nature link
> The human soul that through me ran.

Wordsworth wrote Coleridge (December 24, 1799): "am I fanciful when I would extend the obligation of gratitude to insensate things" (*EY*, p. 275). And we remember that in "Simon Lee" it was the "gratitude of men" (103) which left the poet mourning. Perhaps the turns on gratitude (and ingratitude)—familiar, neighborly, tribal, social—are close to the "theme" of the 1798 *Lyrical Ballads*. We see this idea play in different ways through the treatment of the "Female Vagrant," Goody Blake, Susan Gale, the "Mad

Mother" and the "Old Man Travelling," and it is perhaps not too far fetched to find the concept implied in the other poems. But perhaps what was more important than gratitude itself to Wordsworth were the "links" that produced it, links of man to nature, man to man—which contribute to a universal sense of *being*, and befit songs of thoughtful feeling.

APPENDIX:

Volumes of Poetry

Published in 1798
Seen in This Study

R. Anderson, *Poems on Various Subjects*. Carlisle, 1798. pp. 227.

Joseph Atkinson, *Killarney, A Poem*. Dublin, 1798. pp. 28.

Rev. Luke Booker, LL.D., *Malvern, a Descriptive and Historical Poem*. London, 1798. pp. 124.

Rev. W.L. Bowles, *Coombe Ellen: A Poem*. London, 1798. pp. 27.

Miss Hannah Brand, *Plays, and Poems*. Norwich, 1798. pp. 424.

Joseph Budworth, *Windermere, A Poem*. London, 1798. pp. 28.

Mary Ann Chantrell, of Newington Butts, *Poems on Various Subjects*. London, 1798. pp. 109.

Robert Farren Cheetham, *Poems*. Stockport, 1798. pp. 44.

A Congratulatory Poem on the Escape of Sir Sidney Smith from France, and his Happy Arrival in England. London, 1798. pp. 25.

Joseph Cottle, *Malvern Hills: A Poem*. London, 1798. pp. 71.

Eliza Daye, *Poems, on Various Subjects*. Liverpool, 1798. pp. 258.

Delenda est Carthago; or, a Poetical Paraphrase on the French Declaration. Margate, 1798. pp. 10.

Thomas Dutton, A.M., *The Literary Census: A Satirical Poem*. London, 1798. pp. 117.

[W. Erskin], *Epistle from Lady Grange to Edward D—, Esq.* London, 1798. pp. 24.

Rev. John Chetwood Eustace, *An Elegy to the Memory of the Right Honourable Edmund Burke*. London, 1798. pp. 15.

Joseph Fawcett, *Poems to which are added Civilised War, Before published under the Title of the Art of War, with considerable Alterations*. London, 1798. pp. 277.

The Gardens, a Poem. Translated from the French of the Abbe De Lille. London, 1798. pp. 120.

Thomas Gisborne, *Poems, Sacred and Moral*. London, 1798. pp. 118.

George Goodwin, *Rising Castle, with Other Poems*. Lynn, 1798. pp. 142.

[Thomas Grady], *The Vision, A Poem, Containing Reflections on Fashionable Attachments, Fashionable Marriages, and Fashionable Education. By an Enemy to them All*. Dublin, 1798. pp. 32.

Margaret Holford, *Gresford Vale, and Other Poems*. London, 1798. pp. 44

J. Hucks, A.M., Fellow of Catherine Hall, Cambridge, *Poems*. Cambridge, 1798. pp. 190.

H. Hughes, *Retribution, and other Poems*. London, 1798. pp. 71.

John Hunter, *A Tribute to the Manes of Unfortunate Poets*. London, 1798. pp. 178.

John Jamieson, D.D., F.A.S.S., *Eternity, A Poem: Addressed to Freethinkers and Philosophical Christians*. Edinburgh, 1798. pp. 68.

Jaques, *Satires, &c.* London, 1798. pp. 43.

The Rev. Benj. Johnson, *Original Poems*. Doncaster, [1798]. pp. 223.

Julia; or, Last Follies. London, 1798. pp. 41.

Charlotte and Sophia King, *Trifles of Helicon*. London, 1798. pp. 54.

Edward King, Esq., *Hymns to the Supreme Being. New Edition*. London, 1798. pp. 190.

Poems, By a Lady. London, 1798. pp. 20.

Poems on Various Subjects. By a Lady. London, 1798. pp. 78.

Charles Lloyd and Charles Lamb, *Blank Verse*. London, 1798. pp. 96.

Thomas James Mathias, *Odes, English and Latin. Reprinted 1798. Not published*.

[Thomas Maurice], *The Crisis or the British Muse to the British Minister and Nation. By the Author of Indian Antiquities*. London, 1798. pp. 32.

Elizabeth Moody, *Poetic Trifles*. London, 1798. pp. 186.

Andrew Oedipus, an Injured Author, *The Sphinx's Head Broken: or, a Poetical Epistle*. London, 1798. pp. 14.

The Patrons of Genius: A Satirical Poem. London, 1798. pp. 39.

Peter Pindar, Esq. [John Wolcot], *Tales of the Hoy; interspersed with Song, Ode, and Dialogue*. London, nd [prefixed engraving dated August 1, 1798]. pp. 64.

[Richard Polwhele], *The Unsex'd Females: A Poem, Addressed to the Author of The Pursuits of Literature*. London, 1798. pp. 37.

The Progress of Satire: An Essay in Verse. London, 1798. pp. 32.

Henry James Pye, *Naucratia; or Naval Dominion, A Poem*. London, 1798. pp. 76.

[Samuel Rogers], *An Epistle to a Friend, with other Poems. By the Author of "The Pleasures of Memory."* London, 1798. pp. 47.

The Sea-Side, a Poem, in Familiar Epistles from Mr. Simkin Slenderwit, Summering at Ramsgate, to His Dear Mother in Town. The Second Edition, with great Improvements, and an Appendix. London, 1798. pp. 92.

W. Smyth, Fellow of St. Peter's College, Cambridge, *English Lyrics*. 2nd ed. Liverpool, 1798. pp. 62.

Songs, Duets, Choruses, &c. in the New Musical Piece of The Raft; or, Both Sides of the Water. London, 1798. pp. 14.

Miss Sotheby, *Patient Griselda, A Tale. From the Italian of Boccaccio*. Bristol, 1798. pp. 33.

William Sotheby, Esq., *Oberon, A Poem. From the German of Wieland*. London, 1798.

Miss [Mary R.] Stockdale, *The Effusions of the Heart: Poems*. London, 1798. pp. 160.

Thalia to Eliza: A Poetical Epistle from the Comic Muse to the Countess of D—. London, 1798. pp. 32.

The Wild Huntsman's Chase. From the German of Bürger. London, 1798. pp. 15.

NOTES

Introduction and Conclusion

1. In a note to the poem in the 1800 edition Wordsworth said "it was written with a hope" it had "the principal requisites" of an ode, although he did not so label it. See Chapter Six.

2. *Prose Wks*, I, 124; 139 (see Chapter Seven); *MY*, I, 194. Wordsworth wrote four poems "To the Daisy." The reference here is probably to one of those published in *Poems in Two Volumes* (1807): "In youth" (probably written in 1802), "Bright Flower," and "With little here" (probably written 1802-1805): see Reed, *CMY*, p. 27.

3. For a discussion of what Wordsworth meant by "carrying sensation into the midst of the objects of science itself," see Stephen Prichett, *Coleridge and Wordsworth: The Poetry of Growth* (Cambridge, 1970), pp. 6-21.

4. *The Collected Writings of Thomas DeQuincey*, ed. David Masson (Edinburgh, 1889-1890), X, 48n.

5. They are so dated by Jonathan Wordsworth, *The Music of Humanity: A Critical Study of Wordsworth's Ruined Cottage, incorporating texts from a manuscript of 1799-1800* (London, 1969), p. 188.

6. De Selincourt considers it "quite likely" that the "Prospectus" was written "as early as 1798, at Alfoxden" (*PW*, V, 372); Jonathan Wordsworth dates the material "probably from the end of 1800" (*Music of Humanity*, p. 213); Reed puts it between January 1798 and early 1800 (*CEY*, p. 29).

7. Wordsworth's statement in the Preface, "I have at all times endeavoured to look steadily at my subject" (*Prose Wks.*, I, 132) has sometimes been narrowly interpreted. For correctives, see Frederick A. Pottle, "The Eye and the Object," *Wordsworth Centenary Studies*, ed. Gilbert T. Dunlin (London, 1963), pp. 23-42, and my "Wordsworth's 'Minuteness

and Fidelity'," *PMLA*, LXXII (June 1957), 433-445. See also Chapter Seven.

Chapter One

1. "Wordsworth, Coleridge, and the 'Plan' of the Lyrical Ballads," *Univ. of Toronto Quarterly*, XXXIV (April 1965), 238-253.

2. See Mary Jacobus, "*Peter Bell* the First," *Essays in Criticism*, XXIV (July 1974), 219-242.

3. See my "The Hewing of *Peter Bell*," *Studies in English Literature*, VII (Autumn 1967), 559-603.

4. "My First Acquaintance with Poets" (Howe, XVII, 120).

5. *EY*, p. 194.

6. Coleridge greatly reduced the archaisms in the 1800 edition. See his list of revisions (*Letters*, I, 598-602).

7. *The Prelude* (1805), II, 420-434.

8. Barron Field, *Memoir of the Life and Poetry of Wordsworth*, qtd. *PW*, I, 374. This hitherto unpublished *Memoir* has been announced for publication by the Sydney University Press, edited by Geoffrey Little.

9. *EY*, pp. 125-129, 137-138; 157; *MY*, I, 89. For a full discussion of this collaboration, see Chapter 2, "Partnership," Stephen M. Parrish, *The Art of the Lyrical Ballads* (Cambridge, Mass., 1973).

10. *EY*, p. 189; *The Ruined Cottage* later developed into Book I of *The Excursion*.

11. March 6, 1798 (*EY*, p. 211).

12. *Early Recollections; Chiefly Relating to the late Samuel Taylor Coleridge, During his long residence in Bristol* (London, 1837), I, 309.

13. *EY*, p. 120; ltr. Francis Wrangham (*EY*, p. 159).

14. *EY*, p. 218. Wordsworth also reported returning the borrowed *Zoonomia* of Erasmus Darwin (see note 18 below).

15. *Early Recollections*, I, 299.

16. Griggs (Letters, I, 402) dates "Early April," largely because Coleridge invites Cottle to come for a visit and promises prime scenery if he comes in May; but this need mean no more than while it is still May, and a date in early May for the letter suits better, allowing some time for negotiations. Although not much weight can be put on the fact, Cottle says he received Coleridge's letter at "about the same time" as one from Wordsworth dated May 9 (*Early Recollections*, I, 310).

17. *EY*, pp. 224, 216.

18. *EY*, pp. 191, 192, 198-199. W. told Miss Fenwick that the "incident" of "Goody Blake and Harry Gill" came from Darwin's *Zoonomia*. See the next chapter.

19. *EY*, p. 183; Moorman, I, 297.

20. *EY*, pp. 224, 383.

21. Report to Home Secretary; qtd. Moorman, I, 329.

22. *EY*, pp. 199, 211, 213.

Chapter Two

1. For dating I am indebted, as are all Wordsworthians, to Mark L. Reed, *Wordsworth, The Chronology of the Early Years, 1770-1799* (Cambridge, Mass., 1967).

2. *EY*, pp. 215, 216.

3. Unless, as E.K. Chambers half suggests, Coleridge wrote "The Ancient Mariner" in fourteeners and later divided it (*A Sheaf of Studies* [London, 1942], p. 52).

4. *EY*, pp. 199; 214-215. See Chapter One, notes 14 and 18.

5. For discussion of the curse motif, see Thomas Hutchinson, ed. *Lyrical Ballads, 1798* (London, 1920), xlv, and Emile Legouis, *The Early Life of William Wordsworth, 1770-1798* (London, 1921), pp. 424ff.

6. *PW*, II, 385; *Prose Wks.* I, 118-120. This is the reading of most copies of the 1800 edition; the passage was dropped after 1805.

7. "The Printing of *Lyrical Ballads, 1798,*" *The Library*, 5th ser. Vol IX (December 1954), 221-241. See also George H. Healey, *The Cornell Wordsworth Collection* (Ithaca, 1957), whose notation I follow (p. 3).

8. *Two Lake Poets; a catalogue of printed books, manuscripts and autograph letters by William Wordsworth and Samuel Taylor Coleridge* (London, 1927), p.4. Hutchinson, ed. (*Lyrical Ballads*, pp. x-xiii) develops the anonymity argument.

9. *Letters*, I, 412; *EY*, p. 281.

10. W.J.B. Owen, ed. *Wordsworth and Coleridge Lyrical Ballads, 1798* (Oxford, 1967), p. xviii; Kenneth Currey, *New Letters of Robert Southey* (New York, 1965), I, 176; Foxon ("The Printing of *Lyrical Ballads, 1798,*" p. 237) thinks that the use of a full gathering O suggests that the printer was waiting for more preliminary material.

11. It is even possible that Coleridge wrote the Advertisement: he told William Sotheby (*Letters*, II, 811) that "it was at first intended" that he should write the Preface. Perhaps it is more likely that Wordsworth waited for Coleridge to write the prefatory matter and at the last minute wrote the Advertisement himself, for passages are taken verbatim into the Preface.

12. Whether or not Southey used this copy in preparation of his *Critical Review* article, or was confused about the actual contents of the published volume, is not clear, since he mentioned neither poem in his review; but by December 17, when he wrote to Wynn about *Lyrical Ballads* (Curry, I, 176), he correctly identified Coleridge's contributions, so that he either acquired a later copy or was accurately informed by Cottle.

13. *Early Recollections*, II, 23.

14. Hutchinson, ed., *Lyrical Ballads, 1798*, p. xvi. Hutchinson also suggests that Cottle's name on the title page might have been considered likely to give a lead to the authors' identity (p. xi).

15. Owens, *Lyrical Ballads, 1798*, p. xviii.

16. *EY*, pp. 227; 232.

17. *Letters*, I, 420. Johnson published Coleridge's *Fears in Solitude, Written in 1798, during an Alarm of an Invasion. To which are added, France, an Ode; and Frost at Midnight* (1798).

18. *EY*, pp. 228 and 228n.

19. *EY*, pp. 260; 262n.

20. R.W. Daniel, "The Publication of 'Lyrical Ballads,'" *Modern Language Review*, XXIII (1938), 406-410.

21. Daniel, p. 409; Reed, *CEY*, p. 247.

22. *EY*, pp. 228n, 263. Cottle, however (*Early Recollections*, II, 23) says that he gave "thirty guineas for the Copy-right," and may have considered that part of that sum went to Coleridge. There may also have been advances.

23. Daniel, p. 407n.

Chapter Three

1. [June 7, 1802] *EY*, p. 357. On Wordsworth's language see especially Josephine Miles, *Wordsworth and the Vocabulary of Emotion* (Univ. of California Pub. in English Vol. 12, No.1: 1942) and *Major Adjectives in English Poetry from Wyatt to Auden* (Berkeley, 1946), pp. 317-356.

2. John O. Hayden, (*The Romantic Reviewers*, 1802-1824 [Chicago, 1969], p. 78n) identifies the author of this review, from the staff copy of the British Museum, as the Rev. William Heath.

3. Elsie Smith (*An Estimate of William Wordsworth by his Contemporaries, 1793-1822* [Oxford, 1932]) says the review was "probably" by Wrangham (p. 37); so does Mary Moorman (*William Wordsworth, A Biography: The Early Years, 1770-1803* [Oxford, 1957], p. 486). Neither offers any supporting evidence. Smith also tentatively attributes the *British Critic* review of the second edition of *Lyrical Ballads* (February 1801) to Wrangham, and this double attribution appears to be accepted by Patricia Hodgart and Theodore Redpath, *Romantic Perspectives* (London, 1964), pp. 57-63. Hayden (*The Romantic Reviewers*) does not mention the 1799 review but notes that he has been "unable to discover any indication, much less proof" for the attribution of the 1801 review to Wrangham (p. 79n). The second review seems pretty clearly to have been written by John Stoddart (see ltr. of John Wordsworth to Mary Hutchinson, February 25-26, 1801 (*The Letters of John Wordsworth*, ed. Carl Ketcham [Cornell, 1969], p. 95). The review of the 1798 edition identifies Coleridge as the author of "The Ancient Mariner," and says the reviewer has "not been informed" whether Coleridge also wrote the rest of the volume, but seems to assume he did—which could be a ploy of a friend who knew

Coleridge and Wordsworth and wanted to preserve the sense of a single author suggested by the Advertisement, but still seems a little odd if the reviewer were Wrangham. Don Reiman (*The Romantics Reviewed*, Part A, I, 127) notes merely that this review "was once attributed to Wrangham"; but R.S. Woof ("John Stoddart, 'Michael' and *Lyrical Ballads*," *Ariel*, I [April, 1970], ii, 7-22) says flatly "there is no evidence that Wrangham ever reviewed Wordsworth." Since the second reviewer remarks "we formerly expressed our admiration" of the first volume, it is tempting to speculate that Stoddart might have also been the author of the earlier review; but he appears to rule such a possibility out in a letter to Coleridge on January 1, 1801, in which he claims not to have "dremt of criticizing" until "some three moons wasted" (qtd. by Woof, "John Stoddart . . ."); the "we" may be merely editorial.

4. Benjamin C. Nangle, *The Monthly Review, Second Series, 1790-1815. Indexes of Contributors and Articles* (Oxford, 1955), pp. 9, 159.

5. See Stephen M. Parrish, "Dramatic Technique in the Lyrical Ballads (*PMLA*, LXXIV, 85-97), and *The Art of the Lyrical Ballads* (Harvard University Press, 1973), chapters 3 and 4; Thomas Hutchinson, ed., *Lyrical Ballads, 1798* (London, 1920), pp. 242f.

6. Hayden (*The Romantic Reviewers*, p. 85) identifies the author of the *Annual Review* critique of Wordsworth's *Poems* as Lucy Aikin.

7. In "A Letter to Henry Brougham Esquire" (Brit. Mus. Ad. MS 47890 f. 17); see my "The Hewing of *Peter Bell*" (*Studies in English Literature*, VII, 570).

Chapter Four

1. Raymond D. Havens, "Simplicity, a Changing Concept," *Journal of the History of Ideas*, XIV, 3-32 (*The Simpliciad* quotes herein come from Havens); John F. Danby, *The Simple Wordsworth* (London, 1960); Randall Jarrell, qtd. by Donald Wesling, "The Inevitable Ear: Freedom and Necessity in Lyric Form, Wordsworth and After," *ELH*, XXXVI, 545.

2. Qtd. in Tom Girtin, *Doctor with Two Aunts, a biography of Peter Pindar* (London, 1959).

3. Ltr. to Southey, February 9, 1813 (*Letters*, III, 433); cf. *Biographia Literaria*, Chap. XIV. Coleridge called the Preface "half a child of my own Brain" (ltr. to Southey, July 29, 1802; *Letters*, II, 830); Wordsworth wrote to William Rowan Hamilton that he was "prevailed upon by Mr. Coleridge to write" the Preface (January 4, 1838; *LY*, II, 910).

4. The Author has been identified as William Entfield. See Marjorie L. Barstow, *Wordsworth's Theory of Poetic Diction* (New Haven, 1917), pp. 120ff., and W.J.B. Owen, *Wordsworth's Preface to Lyrical Ballads* (*Anglistica*, IX, 1957), pp. 23ff.

5. *Essays in Criticism, Second Series* (London, 1888), p. 155.

6. Schelling, *5*, 349 (qtd. by E.D. Hirsch, Jr., *Wordsworth and Schelling* [New Haven, 1960], p. 125).

7. *Collected Writings of Thomas De Quincey*, ed. David Masson (London, 1897), X, 229-230. De Quincey appears to be referring to Wordsworth's conversation; a similar idea, however, is expressed in *Essays upon Epitaphs*, III (*Prose Wks.*, II, 84).

Chapter Five

1. Elton, *A Survey of English Literature, 1780-1830* (2 vols.; London, 1912), II, 63; Smith, *An Estimate of William Wordsworth by his Contemporaries* (Oxford, 1932), p. 33.

2. *PMLA*, LXIX (1954), 489.

3. *Wordsworth* (London, 1966), pp. 20-21.

4. Stephen M. Parrish, "Dramatic Technique in the Lyrical Ballads," *PMLA*, LXXIV (1959), 85-97, and *The Art of the Lyrical Ballads* (Harvard University Press, 1973), chapters 3 and 4; Charles Ryskamp, "Wordsworth's *Lyrical Ballads* in Their Time," in *From Sensibility to Romanticism* (New York, 1965), pp. 357-372.

5. *Biog. Lit.*, Chap. IV (Shawcross, I, 50).

6. On the composition and insertion of the "Advertisement," see Chapter Two.

7. *EY*, pp. 310, 337; this letter to Richard was dated 1803 in *Early Letters*, p. 325.

8. *British Critic*, XIV (October 1799), 364; *Critical Review or Annals of Literature*, XXIV (October 1798), 204; *Monthly Mirror Reflecting Men and Manners*, VI (October 1798), 224; *The Cabinet or Monthly Report of Polite Literature*, III (April 1808), 251; *Annual Review and History of Literature*, VI (1808), 523; *Edinburgh Review*, XI (October 1807), 214-15; *Eclectic Review*, IV (January 1808), 35.

9. *De Quincey to Wordsworth*, ed. J.E. Jordan (Berkeley, 1962), p. 28; De Quincey's Collected Writings, ed. D. Masson (London, 1896), II, 129; Mary Gordon, *"Christopher North": A Memoir of John Wilson* (2 vols.; Edinburgh, 1862), I, 40; *The Letters of John Hamilton Reynolds*, ed. L.M. Jones (Lincoln, Neb., 1973), p. 5.

10. *Prose Wks.*, III, 84; W.W. to Sir George Beaumont (*MY*, I, 194). See Patrick Cruttwell, "Wordsworth, the Public, and the People," *Sewanee Review*, LXIV (1956), 71-80.

11. *Notes & Queries*, CCIX (1964), 436-437.

12. *Poetical Register and Repository of Fugitive Poetry for 1804* (London, 1805), p. 493; *Literary Journal, A Review of Literature, Science, Manners, and Politics*, V, (1805), 433; *Poetical Register . . . for 1806-7* (London, 1808), 502.

13. Reviews of *Poems in Two Volumes* in *Monthly Literary Recreations*, XIII (July 1807), 65-66 and *Edinburgh Review*, XI (October 1807), 214.

14. *Annual Review*, I, 657; II, 546-552.

15. *Early Recollections, Chiefly Relating to the Late Samuel Taylor Coleridge, During his long Residence in Bristol* (London, 1837), II, 23, 26-27. See Chapter Two.

16. "Essay, Supplementary to the Preface" (1815: *Prose Wks.*, III, 80; *PW*, II, 426)—W.W. gives Coleridge credit for the idea.

17. The *Poetical Register and Repository of Fugitive Poetry for 1806-7* (London, 1811), pp. 548-549.

18. *Collected Writings*, ed. Masson, I, 14.

19. *Letters*, I, 305; 216.

20. *Literary Hours or Sketches Critical and Narrative* (London, 1798), p. 468.

21. *The Unsex'd Females* (London, 1798), p. 8.

22. *Public Spirit: a Lyric Poem: occasioned by the Exemplary Zeal, Resolution and Decorum, Uniformly manifested by the Yeomanry Corps of Ireland, in the Sacred Cause of their King and Country. To which is prefixed an Address to the Right Hon. Tho. Pelham; And Observations on the Irregular Ode.* Second edition (Dublin, 1797). The copy in the University of Illinois library contains an autograph letter of presentation to Capt. Castle, signed Peter Alley.

Chapter Six

1. Review of *The Patrons of Genius: a Satirical Poem* (1798), VI, 36.

2. *MY*, I, 89. F.T. Swetnam (*Wordsworth's Satiric Voice*, Cornell dissertation, 1967; Dissertation Abstracts 28:2265A) suggests that Wordsworth shifted from satire to humor.

3. Thus the title page; this was William Smyth, Fellow of Peterhouse, who in 1807 became Professor of Modern History. His *English Lyrics* was first published in 1797 and went through five editions.

4. *The Journal of the Rev. William Bagshaw Stevens*, ed. Georgina Galbraith (Oxford, 1965), p. 436.

5. Notes to *Miscellaneous Sonnets* (*PW*, III, 417).

6. Reed, *CEY*, p. 70n.

7. Ltr. to Samuel Rogers, September 29, 1808; *MY*, II, 268; Markham L. Peacock, Jr., *The Critical Opinions of William Wordsworth* (Baltimore, 1950), p. 236.

8. Wordsworth spent much effort revising "Simon Lee," and made changes in the order. See *PW*, IV, 413.

Chapter Seven

1. *Journals of Dorothy Wordsworth*, ed. E. de Selincourt (London, 1952), I, 12-13.

2. *Biog. Lit.*, Chap. XIV (Shawcross, II, 6).

3. *PW*, II, 511; Owen reads "[prominently *del.*] an impressive" (*Wordsworth and Coleridge, Lyrical Ballads 1798* [Oxford, 1967], p. 139).

4. *Biog. Lit.*, Chap. XXII (Shawcross, II, 101); see note 7 to Introduction.

5. Preface, 1802 addition (*PW*, II, 386; *Prose Wks.*, I, 123); "I Wandered Lonely as a Cloud," 21; "Prospectus" to *The Excursion*, 40, and "Tintern Abbey," 100.

6. Ltr. to Samuel Rogers, September 29, 1808 (*MY*, I, 268); "Essay, Supplementary to the Preface" (*PW*, II, 423; *Prose Wks.*, III, 77).

7. F.G. Stephens in "Modern Giants," *Germ*, no. 4 (April 1850), p. 170; Ruskin, *Pre-Raphaelitism* (London, 1851), quoted by William E. Fredeman, "A Key Poem of the Pre-Raphaelite Movement: W.M. Rossetti's 'Mrs. Holmes Grey,'" in *Nineteenth-Century Literary Perspectives* (Durham, N.C., 1974), pp. 149, 156.

8. *PW*, II, 390, 388-389; *Prose Wks.*, I, 132-133, 128-129.

9. Ltr. to unidentified addressee, April 1, 1843 (*LY*, III, 1159).

10. Reed dates as probably from March 19, 1798 (*CEY*, p. 321).

11. *PW*, II, 513. This note appeared in *Lyrical Ballads* 1800-1805. See Introduction.

12. *Biog. Lit.*, II, 6.

13. In a ltr. to William Taylor, January 25, 1800 (*Letters*, I, 566).

14. Stephen M. Parrish, *The Art of the Lyrical Ballads* (Cambridge, Mass., 1973), chapters 3 and 4; *PW*, II, 439; *Prose Wks.*, III, 34.

15. *Henry Crabb Robinson on Books and their Writers*, ed. Edith J. Morley (London 1938), I, 166.

Chapter Eight

1. XVII (February 1801), 131n.

2. O.J. Campbell and Paul Mueschke, "Wordsworth's Aesthetic Development, 1795-1802," *Univ. of Michigan Pub. Lang. & Lit.*, 10 (1933), 22; Stephen M. Parrish, *The Art of the Lyrical Ballads* (Harvard University Press, 1973), chapters 3 and 4. Paul Sheats makes well the point that the ballad form "was both lyrical and objective" (*The Making of Wordsworth's Poetry*, 1785-1798 [Harvard University Press, 1973], p. 280).

3. *EY*, p. 235 and *Letters*, I, 566—this passage comes from correspondence between Wordsworth and Coleridge which the latter transcribed in a letter to William Taylor, January 25, 1800.

4. Sheats, *The Making of Wordsworth's Poetry*, p. 280.

5. *The Complete Works of Walter Savage Landor*, ed. T. Earle Welby (London, 1927), VI, 35; ltr. to J.A. Heraud, November 23, 1830 (*LY*, I, 537).

6. *PW*, II, 401; *Prose Wks.*, I, 150.

7. A version of "The Three Graves" and some unpublished related stanzas partly in the hand of Wordsworth, partly in that of Mary

Hutchinson, appear in the Racedown Notebook; Reed speculates that they were written between November 28, 1796, and June 4, 1797. Wordsworth told Barron Field that he gave Coleridge "the subject of his *Three Graves*"; possibly Wordsworth wrote drafts of Parts I and II (Reed, *CEY*, pp. 189-190; *PW*, I, 374). E.H. Coleridge prints "from an autograph MS" of Coleridge a version of Part II which contains variations, but is substantially the same as that in the Racedown Notebook, and repeats many stanzas verbatim.

8. Kenneth Curry, ed., *New Letters of Robert Southey* (Columbia University Press, 1965), I, 128.

9. *Fors Clavigera*, III, xxxiv, 4.

10. Quoted by Roger Sharrock, "Wordsworth's Revolt against Literature," first printed in *Essays in Criticism*, III (1953); reprinted in *Wordsworth's* Lyrical Ballads, *A Casebook*, ed. A.R. Jones and W. Tydeman (London, 1972), p. 172.

11. *Loc. cit.*

12. Sheats, *The Making of Wordsworth's Poetry*, p. 280; Gérard, *English Romantic Poetry* (University of California Press, 1968), p. 78. See also Thomas L. Ashton, "*The Thorn*: Wordsworth's Insensitive Plant," *Huntington Library Quarterly*, 35: 171-187.

13. See the analysis in Majorie L. Barstow, *Wordsworth's Theory of Poetic Diction* (*Yale Studies in English*, LVII, 1917).

14. *Irrational Man: A Study in Existential Philosophy* (1958; Anchor Books, 1962), pp. 222-223.

15. *EY*, pp. 303-304; *The Monthly Literary Advertiser*, October 10, 1805, p. 45.

16. *The Poetical Works of the Late Mrs. Mary Robinson* (London, 1806), prefaced to "Sir Raymond of the Castle, A Tale"; *Monthly Review*, XXIX (June 1799), 202.

17. Ltrs. to Joseph Cottle, June 2 and June 24 [1799] (*EY*, pp. 263-264); *Lyrical Ballads* (London, 1800), pp. 211f.

18. *English Romantic Poetry*, p. 88.

19. See my essay, "Wordsworth's Humor," *PMLA*, LXXIII (March 1958), pp. 81-93, and Mary Jacobus, "The Idiot Boy," in *Bicentenary Wordsworth Studies*, ed. J. Wordsworth (Cornell, 1970), pp. 238-265.

INDEX

Titles of works are distributed alphabetically, except those of Wordsworth, which are listed under his name.

201